Life Is Long

LIFE

How to Reinvent Your Career

IS

Every Decade

LONG

CHERIE SOYOUNG PAE KLOSS

Published by Forbes Books, Charleston, South Carolina.
An imprint of Advantage Media Group.

Forbes Books is a registered trademark, and the Forbes Books colophon is a trademark of Forbes Media, LLC.

Printed in the United States of America.

10 9 8 7 6 5 4 3 2 1

ISBN: 979-8-88750-503-9 (Hardcover)
ISBN: 979-8-88750-504-6 (eBook)

Library of Congress Control Number: 2024905234

Cover design by Lindsey Bailey.

This custom publication is intended to provide accurate information and the opinions of the author in regard to the subject matter covered. It is sold with the understanding that the publisher, Forbes Books, is not engaged in rendering legal, financial, or professional services of any kind. If legal advice or other expert assistance is required, the reader is advised to seek the services of a competent professional.

Since 1917, Forbes has remained steadfast in its mission to serve as the defining voice of entrepreneurial capitalism. Forbes Books, launched in 2016 through a partnership with Advantage Media, furthers that aim by helping business and thought leaders bring their stories, passion, and knowledge to the forefront in custom books. Opinions expressed by Forbes Books authors are their own. To be considered for publication, please visit **books.Forbes.com.**

To my children, Brandon Kloss and Natalie Kloss,
who have had to weather all the changes in my life
alongside me and were my biggest supporters.

CONTENTS

INTRODUCTION

I'D LIKE TO INTRODUCE YOU TO THREE WOMEN, SARAH, Olivia, and Bree. See if you recognize yourself in any of them.

Sarah is twenty-two. She works a low-wage job she hates but grew up poor and still carries some emotional scars. She doesn't know what she wants to do with the rest of her life. She'd like it to be something cool but doesn't really believe people like her get to have lives like that, so she's waiting tables and surfing a lot.

Olivia has two young kids who seem to need everything all the time. She's always too busy or too tired to think much about her future. Her job is good enough for now, but she knows she'll be miserable if she's still doing the same thing in ten years. She feels like she'd be living for the weekend if the weekend wasn't just more of the same.

Bree's "too good to go" job feels like the proverbial golden handcuffs. She's making great money and doesn't want to rock the boat, but she's bored almost to death and drinking maybe a little more wine than she should to liven things up.

I've been all three of these women and been friends with many more like them. We all could have used a little guidance, but none of us ever saw ourselves in the self-development books that feature privileged women leaning in or taking a couple of years off to eat, pray, and love their way across the globe. But I founded and was CEO of a company that went from making $3 million to $1 billion in two years, and I didn't get there by being another solitary hero on the straight (if torturous) path to success that forms the basis of most rags-to-riches or business success stories. I did it by recognizing three simple truths:

- Life is long. There's more time to do more things than many imagine—and to have a lot of fun doing it!
- Success takes time, but building an interesting career can start immediately.
- Real life can keep some people from following their dreams, but everyone can follow their interests. And when we do, motivation and energy go up, and boredom, depression, anxiety, and resentment go down.

My formula is simple: Recognize we always have two lives—the one we're living and the one we're building. The problem is that most of us are building a future that looks a lot like our present. We're creating something we're already bored with because we've bought into the idea that life is a straight line. We're on a single career *path*. We go from high school to college to an entry-level job to promotion after promotion to retirement to death. A slow rise, a stable plateau, and a steady decline. It's the modern version of an even older progression from apprentice to journeyman to master with apprentices of his own. And yes, *his* own and journey*man*. It's a male model.

But women have always lived our lives in cycles, with each month and with every child, and I believe that puts us in a fantastic position to approach our lives from the perspective of new beginnings and changing cycles. If you think of living your life in a series of ten-year reinvention cycles, you can fit eight lives in there! At fifty-mumble, I still have two more full lives ahead of me. I'm guessing you have at least that many.

That doesn't automatically mean this book is for you. Some people are content and fulfilled on their present life path. I have nothing but respect for that. Maybe you have a strong sense of calling to a career or motherhood. Maybe you know what you were born to do, are doing it now, and hope to do it forever. That's great! You don't need me. But if you're telling yourself this book isn't for you because you're locked into circumstances you can't change, because you didn't get your life off to a great start, because it's already too late, or because too many people depend on you to keep doing what you're doing, I wrote this book for you.

I wrote it for anyone who feels stuck—who wants to break out and try something different but who keeps not doing it. Why don't they "just do it"? Maybe they think their circumstances are locking them in, maybe they're scared, or maybe they think they could summon the courage and get into motion if they just knew where they wanted to go.

I wrote *Life Is Long* for people who want something more, whether they already have quite a lot but still feel restless or have never had much and aren't willing to give up on the idea of getting it.

Finally, I wrote this book for women—not in an exclusionary "no boys allowed" way, but because most books on the personal and career development shelves seem to assume a male reader. Even if the author is a dad, they make recommendations that any mother knows are out of reach for them. If you need to get kids to the school bus with their breakfasts eaten, backpacks packed, and at least most of their clothes on, matched, and right side out, devoting the first three hours of your day to a morning routine of meditation, exercise, deep work, juicing, and day-planning might change your life. But so would a million dollars and a magic wand.

If there was ever anyone who had a reason not to develop personally or professionally, it was me. I grew up poor, a second-generation Korean immigrant with a schizophrenic mother and a dad who abandoned us when I was young. When my mom was institutionalized for mental illness, I was on my own at fifteen, working to pay rent and fitting high school in at the edges. Not exactly what you'd call a setup for success! But I was determined not to be another clichéd drug-dealing inner-city failure facing ten years to life in prison. I was going to create an unexpected future for someone in my circumstances. I reinvented myself. I've done it four times in my life, and I'm working on my fifth.

In 2021, I was named National Entrepreneur of the Year by Ernst and Young—just five years after I started a nurse staffing platform called SnapNurse. I exited the company the following year and started exploring mentorship at scale. Now I'm investing in and advising startups and telling my story here to reach the kind of women who want practical help to create an extraordinary life for themselves. I want to share the steps I took to get where I wanted to be, not in a straight line, but in a series of four-phase cycles, each of which got a little bigger, a little richer, and a lot more interesting with each revolution.

I know there are books out there that say you can mystically manifest abundance, conjure self-belief out of thin air, listen to your heart, or follow your dreams to success, but I won't tell you that you can be anything if you just want it badly enough—because it was always hard for me to hear that kind of advice. I was too disappointed and disillusioned to believe in magic and too well acquainted with how reality gets in the way of dreams. Instead, I'll show you how to build your dream inside your reality, one small piece at a time, because each time you do, your reality gets bigger.

I wasn't trained for big dreams. Certainly, part of that is my gender, generation, and background. I got both the typical first-generation Korean "You're carrying the hopes and aspirations of your parents who gave up everything and worked menial jobs to give you the chance at a better life, so be a good daughter and go into medicine or engineering" and "I hope you get married, and he gets a good job so you can maybe buy a house before your kids leave home." Nobody ever said, "You can build a billion-dollar company one day, write a book, and work in television," but now I've done all three. And I did it all one reinvention and one baby step at a time. You can too.

We'll start with a little test you can take to help you figure out if you're ready for reinvention. I'll explain why I think life is long and careers should be short, and I'll share some of the research that backs me up. Then I'll introduce the ten-year reinvention cycle and look at what might be keeping you stuck. Once you understand the pain, irritability, and boredom of having stayed too long in a phase or between reinvention cycles, you can address the inertia and fears that are keeping you stuck and convert its discomforts into motivation to start moving through the four phases of the reinvention cycle. In each phase, I'll make suggestions for next steps and share examples from my own life and the lives of women I know. We'll start with some courage-building and then take a deeper look at each of the four phases that make up a single ten-year cycle. Here they are:

- **Phase 1.** Discovery
  - Figure out what you want, and explore possible reinventions.

- **Phase 2.** Preparation
  - Evaluate the realism of your reinvention ideas, make a plan, and commit.
- **Phase 3.** Education
  - Learn what you need to know, and gain enough experience to start living your reinvention.
- **Phase 4.** Achievement
  - Enjoy your success, and start looking forward to your next reinvention.

Every one of my reinvention cycles was kicked off or kept going by other women—from the friend who launched me on my first search for a more meaningful future to the pact I made with my fellow anesthetists to the support I got from my mother-in-law when I was working two jobs and starting SnapNurse. I didn't do it alone. You don't have to either. If you want something more or feel stuck, inadequate, bored, or scared, I wrote this book for you. I wrote it because I'm reinventing myself again as I write it. Let's do it together.

Chapter 1

WHERE ARE YOU? (AND WHERE'S MY EUCALYPTUS?)

I WAS FORTY-NINE AND STILL WORKING A PART-TIME JOB when I started SnapNurse. As it ramped up, I was running ragged. I wasn't getting enough sleep, I was eating like a college kid, and I barely had time to shower. I gained fifty pounds. (Constantly eating to stay energized, lack of sleep, and stress can add up to some serious weight issues.) One day, I was working from home to save the twenty-minute commute when my neighbor sent me an angry text. Apparently, the gardeners had blown some of "my" leaves onto *her* lawn. She was outraged. My leaves had ruined her day! (As a point of fact, the leaves had fallen from *her* trees onto *my* lawn, but I was too busy to care. I'm not sure I had even noticed it was fall.) I remember thinking, *How boring and empty does your life have to be to let a few leaves upset you so much?*

I thought of her again years later. I'd recently exited Snap-

Nurse and was taking some time off to recover from the madness and indulge myself a little. I'd just finished a workout and was looking forward to a nice steam. The sauna at my spa squirts eucalyptus on the walls to give the air that bracing menthol tang that feels like it'll snake down into your lungs and scour them clean. It's nice. This time, I checked before I went in because the last time I was there, they'd just cleaned out the room and not yet replenished the eucalyptus.

There was not a whiff of eucalyptus.

A flash of anger surged through me. *Why was there no eucalyptus?* I had mentioned it to the front-desk lady the other day, and she'd given me that too-sunny smile that meant she'd instantly forget what I said, *and* I'd had to walk by the desk three times before I found her.

I stomped down the hall—on the warpath in my fuzzy robe and slippers. That's when I remembered my neighbor. The lack of eucalyptus in the steam room had ruined my day.

I had my answer to the question I'd asked myself as I tried to appease my neighbor about the leaves—pretty darn empty. I'd turned into an Asian Karen. I had a good laugh at myself, but then I turned introspective. I realized I was bored and lacking purpose.

There are three bits of good news to this embarrassing story: I recognized that emptiness for what it was, knew what to do about it, and didn't inflict the manager-calling and Google-review-writing vengeance I'd been plotting.

WHERE I WAS

My spa rest-and-relaxation wasn't restful or relaxing because I'd overstayed my time in the fourth phase of the reinvention cycle. Each of the phases has its own work and warning signs, and irrational irritability is one I've learned to watch for.

Warning signs start going off when you've stayed too long in one phase of the cycle or when you're not doing its work either because you're scared or you don't know what that work is. Some warning signs are universal, but most look at least subtly different depending on the phase. Irritability is a universal sign. I was able to recognize the variant I manifested at the spa (let's call it Karening) because retrospection—looking back over your life—is part of that phase's work.

WHERE ARE YOU?

In this chapter, we'll inventory the warning signs that show up when you stay too long in one of the four phases or when you stall out between the end of one ten-year cycle and the start of the next. I call that between-cycles stuck space Phase o because it's empty, and every one of the warning signs waves its red flag when you're there. So here's an inventory of the warning signs to help you determine where you are.

ARE YOU IRRITABLE?

When little things get in your way, do you roll right over them or stop and fixate? Are you cranky and impatient, snapping at strangers and making the people close to you miserable? I've learned to recognize irritability as one of the earliest warning signs that I'm getting restless. Even when working two jobs and being exhausted, I'm more tolerant of little annoyances than I am when I'm bored.

1. Is it all starting to get on your nerves?

IS THE FUN FUN?

After college, I got a job teaching science at a private school. The pay wasn't great, so I kept my old restaurant job waiting tables, but even working two jobs, I found time to get down to the ocean at least twice a day to surf. Surfing may just be the perfect flow-generating activity. Everything about it seems designed to make you feel great. Surfing never stopped being fun, but it got empty. After three years of looking forward to grabbing my board and hitting the beach, I started to think about going down to the water and asking myself, *Why bother?* Sure, it would be a good time, but it would be a good time just like yesterday and tomorrow, and it wasn't as rewarding as it used to be anyway.

When I started working in TV, I was having so much fun that the work didn't feel like work. I'd glance up from editing a tape and be stunned that it was midnight. I was thrilled to produce TV concepts and show my tapes to network execs. Seven years later, I was arguing with a reality TV star on one of my shows like a stereotypical Hollywood a**hole. I was refusing advice from other producers and felt generally dissatisfied with every tape we produced. I didn't want to leave something I had worked so hard to get, but it wasn't fun anymore.

My husband and I divorced when our youngest was three years old, so I was a working single mom for most of their lives, but I have friends who stayed home with their kids and loved it. They felt deeply fulfilled watching their babies grow, but when the kids left for college, they'd turn to me and whisper, "If I have to do another day of ladies, Pilates, and complaining about our husbands over vodka martinis, I'm going to lose my mind." Playing pickleball with vodka in your thermos is probably not the most rewarding way to live as an empty nester.

2. Is the fun rewarding?

HOW'S YOUR ENERGY?

After my spa-day realization that my self-care was sabotaging my mental health, I started advising up-and-coming entrepreneurs—mostly women—as part of my next reinvention cycle. It wasn't a service I'd charge for. I just found that people kept reaching out to me for advice, so I formalized it a bit. I'd meet folks for breakfast, let them tell me about their startups, and share my thoughts with them. Sometimes, one of them would make a pitch for financial backing, and if I thought they were onto something good, I'd make a modest investment.

The last pitch I got was from a young woman who told me about her business and then mentioned that another company had made her a job offer. She would have to close her startup business if she took the new job. I asked her how she felt about that, and she poked at her egg sandwich. "Oh, I don't know," she sighed. "It's been three years, and I've tried so many things, and nothing's worked, so maybe?"

I recognized that burned-out sigh. She had a good idea, and I thought the business had a real chance, but it was never going to make it if its founder didn't have any more energy than that. This poor woman was rung dry. And the fact that she was even considering other options meant she had one foot out the door already.

I usually meet entrepreneurs earlier in the game, and their eyes are feverishly bright. They can't sit still. They're done with their entrees before I've finished my coffee. They will max out every credit card, beg every relative for a loan, and sleep on someone's couch until they either run out of money or become successful. They'll never consider taking a full-time job until they've tried everything.

I saw the same kind of creative energy when I was working in reality TV. Some producers couldn't wait to collaborate. They wanted to talk about the pitches. "What if she said this instead of that?" "What if we did this in addition to that?" Everyone worked together because they were excited about the project they shared and felt their contribution could make a difference. Every little tweak might make the collective better. They had a passion for their work, and it kept the fire in them alive.

3. Are you dry or on fire?

There's rung dry and on fire, and then there's stomped flat. The entrepreneur I met for breakfast felt deflated, but she was still restless. On the far side of where she was, the landscape levels out and turns gray. When energy isn't just at a low ebb but gone altogether, when breakfast tastes like ash, and when nothing can stir up a spark, you've gone beyond demotivation and into depression.

4. Are you depressed?

ARE YOU BORED?

Being bored comes in three different flavors: same, easy, and meh.

When there's very little variation in what you do every day, time doesn't have enough texture to catch and hold your attention. Every patient I monitored as an anesthetist was different and having a different operation with a different doctor, but the beep-beep-beep of the heart rate monitors was always the same. I worked very hard and sacrificed a lot to land that job, but I quickly got bored with it.

People vary in their need for variation. If you (like me) bore easily, recognize that you'll start seeing this warning sign very early unless you're deliberate about finding a job with a high degree of variety built in. Project-based jobs are a great way to solve this problem. I never faced this kind of boredom while I was working in TV. Every new show I pitched was different, with different storylines and different characters in different situations and places. I got sick of TV, but I was never same-bored.

5. Are you same-bored?

For a while, I worked for a battered women's shelter with houses in secret locations to protect the women from their abusers. Four families lived in each house, and I went back and forth between two of them. I cooked, cleaned, and made sure the residents ate and did their chores. It was fulfilling work, but it wasn't challenging. I could almost feel my brain starting to atrophy. I was easy-bored.

I eventually got easy-bored with anesthesiology too. The work was initially challenging, but with years of practice, I got good at it. When the difficulty of something outstrips your ability, it's incredibly stressful, but when your abilities significantly exceed the difficulty level—even if that level is objectively high—it gets boring.

6. Are you easy-bored?

Meh-boredom comes when you just don't care. (The HR term for it is "disengagement.") It's what happens when you feel like your work doesn't matter. There's no sense of purpose or meaning behind it and no sense of pride or fulfillment coming from it.

7. Are you meh-bored, or disengaged?

Finally, there's an advanced form of boredom that happens if you've been very bored for a very long time. Your brain starts to go a little mushy. After ten years in anesthesiology, when I got home at night and my kids asked how my day was, I couldn't remember. I knew I'd done anesthesia for the last ten hours, but the only days that stood out as memorable were the really bad ones—the kind of days you want to forget. A brilliant moment in the movie *While You Were Sleeping* captures this level of extreme boredom beautifully. Sandra Bullock's character works all day as a subway toll token collector, or as she puts it, "Every day I go, and I sit in a booth like a veal."

8. Are you a veal in a box?

ARE YOU BORING?

There are two varieties of boring: busy-boring and bored-boring.

Some people are always busy but never actually do much. Being busy does not equal being productive. Busy-boring people fill their days with mundane tasks to avoid making the life changes needed to escape their boredom.

9. Are you busy-boring?

Bored-boring is harder to spot, and no one will tell you directly (although they will stop inviting you to do things). Bored-boring is what happens when you're so bored for so long that uninteresting things start to interest you. Bored-boring people burrow down into the mundane minutiae of their lives and then want to tell you about it. They will give you a blow-by-blow account of the PTA meeting or of their daughter's sleepover party.

10. Are you bored-boring?

HOW'RE YOUR MORNINGS?

Starting when I was fifteen, I took the bus from school straight to my job in a bakery, worked until bedtime, slept, and took the bus back to school. I did all my homework on those two-a-day hour-long bus rides. There wasn't much time to get into ordinary teenage trouble. There was less time to sleep. I woke up tired but didn't struggle to get out of bed. I couldn't miss the bus.

Those early years were a preview of what my mornings would be like for much of my life. When I was in grad school, I never got enough sleep, but when the alarm went off, my feet hit the ground. The same was true for the early days of Snap-Nurse. I was so excited to have my own startup that I'd roll out of bed every Friday at 4:00 a.m. to do payroll, and it still didn't feel like work.

I've also had periods when I woke up rested but couldn't get out of bed. I'd lie there, too full of emptiness to get up and do it all again. I was getting plenty of sleep but didn't wake up energized. By 2022, SnapNurse was firmly established. After five years of break-neck growth, things were finally starting to stabilize. I can't say I was caught up on sleep yet, but bone-deep exhaustion wasn't the first sensation I felt upon opening my eyes. It was dread. I'd lie in bed feeling my phone on the bedside table like an undetonated bomb waiting to eviscerate me with the emails, complaints, and problems that came in all day and built up while I slept.

11. Do you wake up tired or dreading the day?

ARE YOU UNDERPAID?

Teaching was probably the most rewarding career I've had, but those rewards were strictly nonmonetary. The work was interesting, and I enjoyed the kids. I got to teach different kinds of science and come up with fun experiments. I would happily have continued teaching, but it paid so little that I had to keep waitressing at night to cover my expenses.

I went into anesthesiology almost exclusively for the money. And the money was great! I spent the first couple of years marveling at how rich I was. But eventually, the money wasn't enough to make up for the boredom and the lack of respect. Even though I was making more than I'd ever made by a factor of three, it still wasn't enough to put up with that job.

Not making enough money is stressful, but not making what you're worth adds a layer of insult to stress, and that can take a heavy emotional toll. I felt this to a certain extent while doing anesthesiology, but I see it even more in women who've made significant career sacrifices to stay home with their kids. If you're unpaid or underpaid to the point that you feel taken advantage of, angry, or resentful, or if your lack of appropriate financial compensation is starting to drag your self-esteem, you're not just underpaid; you're insulted.

12. Do you feel underpaid or insulted?

ARE YOU UNDEREMPOWERED?

Before going to Emory to become an anesthetist, I tried out nursing school. It didn't take long to figure out I wasn't a good fit for nursing. I grew up scrappy, having to fend for myself, and I knew things were going to go badly if doctors treated me the way they treated nurses. Contrary to the stereotype of Asian females, I'm willing to speak my mind loudly. So loudly that sometimes (okay, more than sometimes), I get myself in trouble.

Nurses are caring, smart, educated people, but the system and the power players within it rarely show them the respect they deserve. Even the ones with years of experience still need a doctor's order to give a Tylenol. Years later, running SnapNurse, I had to constantly fight for the nurses' working conditions and pay. I know how hard the nurses work, and I admire their dedication to the practice. It's so much harder than people realize! (Nurses put up with harsh working conditions and so much disrespect from their managers, patients, and doctors, which is why they're leaving the profession in droves.)

13. Are you underempowered?

HOW DOES TIME FLY?

Of course, if you're Groucho Marx, time flies like an arrow, and fruit flies like a banana. For the rest of us, time sometimes flies like an arrow and sometimes crawls like a stoned turtle with a broken leg. When I was getting SnapNurse off the ground, hours went by so quickly that I could barely keep up. Ten years into my anesthesiology career, the minutes limped along. Every shift seemed five hours longer than it should have been.

14. Does your time at work crawl, walk, run, or sprint?

The longer I stayed in anesthesiology, the slower time moved. Every day felt like the last and the next. When I talked to my work friends about it, they felt the same, but they felt stuck. For them, time had stopped—or at least been suspended—while they raised their kids or until they felt like they could leave such a good salary. I knew I wasn't stuck, but I vividly remember how heavy the brakes felt. Stalling out in the familiar, safe, high-paying rut was a real temptation. If I'd stopped, I would have been stuck too.

15. Are you feeling stuck?

WHERE YOU ARE

If you answered yes to all or even the majority of the fifteen questions above, you're probably ready to start a new ten-year reinvention cycle. If only some of the descriptions seem to fit, you may have stayed too long in one of the discovery, preparation, education, and creation phases. Either way, *Life Is Long* can help you. If you answered "no" to most of the questions, put the book down and enjoy your life—it sounds like you're already in the right place!

CHAPTER SUMMARY

If you're irritable and finding you no longer enjoy what you used to do for fun; if you're feeling burned out, bored, and boring; if you wake up not wanting to get out of bed and feel underpaid and underempowered; and if time seems stuck or to just drag by, it's a warning sign that you need to keep (or get) a reinvention cycle moving.

Chapter 2

THE TEN-YEAR REINVENTION CYCLE

THINK BACK TO THE LAST TIME YOU TOOK A BIG VACATION. You probably spent hours figuring out where you wanted to go, shopping for deals, and making reservations. If you're like most people I know, although that work can be tedious, it was probably also enjoyable. You could imagine yourself in exciting new places, engaged in activities that exhilarate or relax you, depending on the kind of vacation you like to have. Anticipation is fun!

Now, remember what it was like to leave the house and start your big trip. Maybe it was a little hectic, even a bit scary, but you got to the airport, dealt with logistics, and then, there you were! Suddenly, you were there in the places you'd imagined being, and doing what you'd dreamed of doing. It was great for days, maybe weeks. Then it probably all started to get just that little bit exhausting. Maybe you found yourself not looking forward to the next museum, or you ended up a little sunburned from lying on the beach too long. Maybe the exotic food started to upset your digestion. You started to look forward to getting back home.

THE TEN-YEAR REINVENTION CYCLE

There's no absence of advice or lack of evidence in favor of reinventing your life every decade. What's missing is an actionable, practical plan that doesn't assume you have enough money to take years off as you do a second residency while someone else takes care of the kids. We'll start by taking a high-level look at some of the research on: why most people start getting bored with their careers between five and seven years into them, how changing our anticipated career length lowers the stakes, why our interests and abilities change over time, and what staying too long in a field does to your ability to make a significant contribution to it. Then I'll introduce the four phases of the ten-year reinvention cycle and explain why each is important to a long (and interesting) life.

WHY WE GET BORED

Almost anything—even the perfect two weeks away that you've saved up for and looked forward to—gets old after a while. People who win the lottery or lose a limb get used to their new circumstances surprisingly quickly.[1] How much more likely is it that your career—even one you went through years of education to get and loved doing—will start to feel routine after a

---

1   Philip Brickman, Dan Coates, and Ronnie Janoff-Bulman, "Lottery Winners and Accident Victims: Is Happiness Relative?" *Journal of Personality and Social Psychology* 36, no. 8 (1978): 917–927, https://doi.org/10.1037//0022-3514.36.8.917.

few years on the job? According to a *Bloomberg Businessweek* article, experts found that after ten years, everyone was bored with their position and recommended shuffling them around within the organization to keep them from leaving.[2] I also found that 50 percent of workers wanted to change jobs, no matter how recently they'd been hired.[3]

Evolutionary psychologists who research boredom theorize it's an adaptive trait designed to keep us from getting too comfortable for too long. Our species might not have survived without a biologically programmed need for newness. It certainly wouldn't have tried eating oysters or taken to the ocean on rafts. In other words, boredom is evolutionarily designed to be painful—so painful, in fact, that people would rather give themselves electric shocks than sit quietly in a room with their thoughts.[4] Boredom exists to prompt us to "pursue a goal that appears to us to be more stimulating, interesting, challenging, or fulfilling than the goal that we currently pursue."[5]

LOWER THE STAKES

I've seen this play out in my own life and the lives of my friends, but I'm not the only one who's noticed it. Dr. Nassir Ghaemi—a psychiatrist, the director of the Mood Disorder Program at Tufts

---

2   Arianne Cohen, "Why You Should Quit Your Job After 10 Years," *Bloomberg Businessweek*, June 24, 2022, https://www.bloomberg.com/news/articles/2022-06-24/make-a-career-change-every-10-or-so-years-experts-say.

3   Abigail Johnson Hess, "'The Great Reimagination of Work': Why 50% of Workers Want to Make a Career Change," *CNBC Make It*, October 12, 2021, https://www.cnbc.com/2021/10/12/why-50percent-of-workers-want-to-make-a-career-change-new-survey.html.

4   Timothy D. Wilson et al., "Just Think: The Challenges of the Disengaged Mind," *Science*, vol. 345, no. 6192 (2014): 75–77, https://doi.org/10.1126/science.1250830.

5   Sara Chodosh, "There's a Right and Wrong Way to be Bored," *Popular Science*, January 22, 2021, https://www.popsci.com/story/science/boredom-benefits/.

Medical Center, and a Harvard Medical School lecturer—is on my side. In a recent *Psychology Today* article entitled "Why You Should Change Your Life Every Decade," he observes that his college-aged daughter and her peers suffer from what he calls a "paralysis in commitment." He ascribes this inability to pick a major to their mistaken belief that "they have to decide what they are going to do 'for the rest of their lives.'" Ghaemi suggests that not only are they right that they don't know what they'll want for so many decades but that "they shouldn't even think about doing something for the rest of their lives. They should just focus on the next ten years. And then after that, if they are very successful, they should quit what they are doing and focus on another ten years."[6]

He explains why. "Whether they succeed or fail, they should plan on making a change every decade or so. Too often, we think we should make a change only if things aren't going well or if we are failing in some way. That is so. But we don't realize we should make changes even when we succeed. The problem is that failure tends to be seen as a good reason to make a change, but people will think there's something odd if you want to make a change because of, or despite, success. Yet it really doesn't matter. Either way, you should make a change because either way, things might turn out better than they are if you make that change. And you'll never know until you do."[7]

OUR CHANGING BRAINS

Harvard professor Arthur Brooks suggests changing careers every decade because our brains and intelligence change as we

---

6   Nassir Ghaemi, "Why You Should Change Your Life Every Decade," *Psychology Today*, posted January 24, 2023, https://www.psychologytoday.com/intl/blog/mood-swings/202301/the-ten-year-rule-change-your-life-every-decade.

7   Ghaemi, "Why You Should Change."

age. The kind of thinking that made you good at one job in your twenties will be on the decline by your forties, but a different kind of intelligence will be on the ascendency.[8]

Brooks has lived his life accordingly. He was a professional musician for his first ten-year cycle, during which he started taking online courses, moved into his second cycle, got a PhD in economics, and became a professor. The next cycle saw him working as the head of the American Enterprise Institute for ten years, during which he wrote his first book. As part of his current cycle, he's written several more, started a popular podcast, and become something of a happiness guru.

THE COST OF EXPERIENCE

In a more altruistic vein, David Sackett, an expert in patient compliance, realized that it was reliably the relative newcomers to a field and not the decades-established experts who did the most to advance it. He "wrote a paper calling for the compulsory retirement of experts and never again lectured, wrote, or refereed anything to do with compliance."[9] Twenty years after his initial training as a medical school professor, he repeated his residency because he "wasn't a good enough doctor."[10]

Sackett then went on to become the father of evidence-based medicine, spearheading a fundamental change in medical decision-making.[11] Realizing he'd once again become an expert,

---

8   Arthur C. Brooks, *From Strength to Strength: Finding Success, Happiness, and Deep Purpose in the Second Half of Life* (New York: Portfolio, 2022).

9   David L. Sackett, "The Sins of Expertness and a Proposal for Redemption," *BMJ*, vol. 6, no. 320 (2000): 1283, https://www.ncbi.nlm.nih.gov/pmc/articles/PMC1118019/.

10   "Obituaries: David Sackett," *BMJ*, vol. 350, no. 8009 (2015), https://doi.org/10.1136/bmj.h2639.

11   David M. Eddy, "The Origins of Evidence-Based Medicine: A Personal Perspective," *AMA Journal of Ethics*, vol. 13, no. 1 (2013): 55–60, https://doi.org/10.1001/virtualmentor.2011.13.1.mhst1-1101.

he announced he had "decided to get out of the way of the young people now entering this field and will never again lecture, write, or referee anything to do with evidence-based clinical practice." And that was it. He started what he called his eighth career, studying randomized clinical trials, which he found "as challenging and exhilarating as its predecessors."[12]

FOUR PHASES AND THE IN-BETWEEN

Rather than having multiple, successive careers as Ghaemi, Brooks, and Sackett did, we'll build a more gradual cycle in which the next thing emerges during the first, and only gradually separates from it to become its own new thing. In our model, rather than an abrupt stop and new start, day bleeds into night, which fades back into day.

The four phases of the ten-year reinvention cycle are a bit like the phases of the moon, but what rises and ebbs is commitment and energy. We start in the dark of the moon, where there's little excitement or change. This first (and final) Phase 0 is painful. Many people encounter it for the first time when the life plan that began with "when I grow up, I'm going to be a..." runs out of steam or into reality. Most of us get a little lost when this happens. This phase recurs with the pain of boredom that sets in (according to both my research and my personal experience) after between five to seven years in the same job. Finally, it's the pain of disappointment when a planned reinvention goes down in flames or short-circuits.

In this phase, the pain, irritability, and boredom you're feeling are warning signs that it's been too long since you've started a new (or your first) reinvention cycle. Your work in Phase 0 is to

---

12 Sackett, "The sins of expertness."

figure out what's keeping you stuck and to get the cycle moving again. Because this work is probably the most emotionally if not physically taxing of any in the ten-year reinvention cycle, it gets two chapters. Because this is a cycle, it's where we end up and where we begin.

Once you've understood why it's worth the work, gotten yourself unstuck, and gathered your courage, life starts getting a little brighter. Phase 1 begins with a tiny new-moon sliver of hope as you look for what you want and explore its possibilities.

As you start figuring out what you want and researching what you'd need to do to get it, interest and excitement grow, and you enter Phase 2 with a commitment and a plan. In this phase, you gather knowledge and collect experience so that by the time you hit the full-moon intensity of Phase 3, you're ready to give it everything you've got.

Phase 4 begins when you've reached your goal. This is the time to enjoy your success and ride the wave as far as it will take you, knowing it won't last. But you've learned to watch for the warning signs and don't get stuck in Phase 0 again. Instead, you start finding the next dream as the energy of the current one wanes. Then you head into your next reinvention.

Like most young people, I thought about my future career as a straight line—a path, not a cycle. I decided early on that I was going to be a doctor and took a science-intensive premed load of AP classes in high school. My single-track plan derailed in college, where I graduated premed but without the impressive GPA I'd need to get into top-tier medical schools.

I went to my college career counselor for advice. In 1988 at a 1300-person conservative Christian college, that advice was "If you're interested in medicine, be a nurse."

"But I want to be a doctor."

"Be a nurse. It's so much easier, and the lifestyle is better for when you get married and have a family."

I don't think he was being misogynistic. I think he thought I was overly ambitious and that he was protecting me from myself. I was young and didn't have any parental guidance, and all my friends who weren't going into teaching were going into nursing, so that's where I went. Med school? I didn't even apply, and there I was, at twenty-two, deep in the dark of Phase 0.

CHAPTER SUMMARY

There are compelling, research-backed reasons to reinvent your life every decade. Our natural, adaptive tendency toward boredom means most people start to get restless after five years in the same job, and thinking about our careers in terms of shorter time commitments makes us less afraid to try things out. Even if we're successful in our jobs, our interests and abilities change over time, and success itself may impede our ability to do great work. In short, most careers slow and eventually end a growth cycle most don't know they have.

Recognizing that there's a cycle of discovery, preparation, education, and achievement allows you to have multiple professional lives in your one long life. But it isn't easy, so let's look at the benefits of living your life in a series of ten-year reinvention cycles.

Chapter 3

WHAT'S IN IT FOR YOU?

I'D KNOWN ELSA FOR YEARS. WE'D MET AT EMORY AND worked together as anesthetists after graduating, so I was surprised when I walked into her bedroom during a party and found her staring into space. I asked what was wrong, and Elsa said she felt stuck and extremely bored. She had a nice career, husband, house, and two great, straight-A kids and was very busy with work and family. I didn't understand her melancholy or boredom. I sat down next to her. "I have a good life," Elsa told me without looking up. "We go on vacation every year and..."

She trailed off. I waited. She finally met my eyes. "It just isn't enough. I'm busy; I get up every morning at 6:30; I work until 3:00; from 3:00 to 7:00, Ashley has cheerleading, and Amy has band. Then I cook dinner and do the dishes, and it's the same thing every day. It's too much, and it isn't enough!"

I'd known Elsa was unhappy; she was always complaining about something her husband or one of the girls had done, but I didn't realize how much her life felt like *Groundhog Day*.

"I think I'm depressed," she told me.

I didn't think so. I'm not dismissing mental illness when I say that. There absolutely are people whose neurochemistry underlies serious emotional pain and disrupts their lives—my mother was one of them—but I didn't think Elsa was depressed. I thought she needed to reinvent herself.

"Want to come work with me at my startup?" I suggested.

"I can't. I..." Elsa stopped. "Yeah," she said. "What the hell! I really do!"

We didn't know it then, but neither of us would have anything like a normal day again for a long time. Elsa joined SnapNurse just before the pandemic turned everything in our lives and the entire field of nursing on its head, and I honestly don't know if I would have made it through without her on board. She threw herself into the work and moved up through the ranks quickly. She was always my friend, but she was also a stellar employee. And she loved all of it.

We threw Elsa a fiftieth birthday party a year later at a nice restaurant with her friends and family present. Her daughters gave her a card that read, "We're so proud of you, Mom!"

Her husband stood up and gave a moving toast thanking Elsa for being the amazing person she was. He thanked their kids and her parents. And then he said, "So thank you to Elsa for making me a better man, and thank you to SnapNurse for making Elsa a better person." Everyone laughed, but he wasn't done. "You know, when Elsa was working in anesthesiology, she'd come home from work and start complaining or picking on us. Now, she's just happy to sit down with us. She knows what she's doing is important, and it makes her so much more patient with all the little things."

Elsa raised her glass. "It's true!" she agreed. "I've completely reorganized my priorities in the last two years and gotten out of my rut. My work is fulfilling, and I love working with my best friends."

WHAT'S IN IT FOR YOU?

In this chapter, I'll make my argument for the claim I set out in this book's title that life is long and talk through the implications of accepting that as true. Then I'll explain why I think breaking that long life into a series of ten-year reinvention cycles is the smartest and most interesting way of approaching that long life by exploring what's in it for you.

LIFE IS LONG

When I was young, life felt like it hurtled along at a break-neck speed. I don't think it feels any slower to young people today. If anything, things seem even more rushed. There's so much pressure on you to finish high school so you can get to college. There's a sense that if you don't get your life started in your twenties, you will have permanently and irrevocably missed the proverbial boat. I mean, how are you going to climb the corporate ladder the whole way through your thirties and forties if you're not already clambering along by the time you're twenty-five?

I've seen friends push their kids to skip grades so they could put high school behind them by fifteen or sixteen and head off to Harvard. I think some of them would skip childhood altogether if they could, just to get a jump start on work. I don't get it. Yes, we live in a capitalist society. Yes, earning money is important, but so are life experiences and friendships.

In addition to my grades and my college counselor's influence, another reason I didn't go to med school was that I ran the numbers and thought, *Twelve more years of education means I'll be ancient—thirty-three—before my life even really starts!*

If I'd realized then how long life is, I could have done some additional math. The average age of retirement for doctors is sixty-eight, so I could have had a career that was longer than I would have been old when I started—thirty-five years.[13]

I didn't realize how long life was until I hit my forties doing anesthesia and thought, *Hang on, I still have twenty-five more years before I reach retirement age. What if I'm so miserable I end up dying before I get there?* I had medical training, after all. I knew being unhappy was bad for your health.[14]

Back in the days when your profession was mostly determined by your gender and what your dad did for a living, it made sense for a blacksmith, a farmer, or a king to do the same job until he died. At thirty-two.[15] You only had one career because life was short.

It isn't anymore. At 76.4 years, life expectancy in the US is now more than twice what it used to be, so I think it's past time to move away from the idea that you can only do one thing until you die.[16] Even if you do one job until you retire at sixty-three, you could still go to law school and have a ten-year career before you hit seventy-six (at which point, you would still expect to live

---

13 Naveed Saleh, "Physicians Put Off Retirement: Here's Why," May 3, 2022, Rama On Healthcare, https://ramaonhealthcare.com/physicians-put-off-retirement-heres-why/.

14 Elizabeth M. Lawrence, Richard G. Rogers, and Tim Wadsworth, "Happiness and Longevity in the United States," *Social Science & Medicine*, vol. 145, November (2015): 115–119, https://doi.org/10.1016/j.socscimed.2015.09.020.

15 Maria Patrizia Carrieri and Diego Serraino, "Longevity of Popes and Artists between the 13th and the 19th Century," International Journal of Epidemiology, vol. 34, no. 6 (2005): 1435–1436, https://doi.org/10.1093/ije/dyi211. According to Wikipedia, average life expectancy used to be 32.2 years, assuming you made it to age ten, which at least a third didn't. Wikipedia, accessed November 1, 2022, https://en.wikipedia.org/wiki/Life_expectancy.

16 FastStats, US Life Expectancy, Centers for Disease Control and Prevention, last reviewed February 7, 2023, https://www.cdc.gov/nchs/fastats/life-expectancy.htm.

another seven years). Ten years is a long time to be in a career. I grew SnapNurse from nothing to a $1 billion company in six.

I think one thing that contributes to our tendency to think of the first profession we choose as a lifetime commitment comes from a more general sense that things in the world are permanent—but they're not. It gives us a sense of security, even of control, but it's illusory. Life can change in a heartbeat. Luck can pay off or run out overnight.

Day to day, things may look the same, but if you take a minute and think about how different your days were ten years ago, you can see the scale of change. I'm writing this early in 2023. In 2013, if I'd told you that a pandemic would practically shut the world down and change the way everyone worked, with TV anchors reporting from their bedrooms and almost seven million dead, would you have believed me?

Of course, you might reasonably argue that COVID-19 was an outlier event. Sure. But go back another ten years, and there was no LinkedIn, Skype, Myspace, Facebook, Twitter, Spotify, or iPads. The explosion of social media and the 2008 global recession changed quite a lot about the way we work in those ten years.

The average age of death today is almost eighty. Someone who dies at that age today was born before the first transistor and in an entirely different era—the Second Industrial Revolution—when the most advanced technology was mechanical and analog.

Even without factoring in the impact of AI, considering how much dramatically changes in a single decade, if you work for only half of your projected life expectancy, you can reasonably expect to see a lot of change. To my way of thinking, life is long, and change is inevitable. It might as well be interesting!

In the Introduction, I said that if you were happy in your

current work and weren't looking to change things up, this book probably wasn't for you. That's not because I don't think change isn't headed your way. It is. It's just that if you're not curious or restless or interested in having an interesting life, I'm not here to change your mind. If, on the other hand, you want an interesting life, a mindset shift is in order.

THE MINDSET SHIFT

When you start thinking of life as long, you start looking at time as something to invest rather than spend. When I decided not to go to medical school, part of what I was thinking was *I don't want to waste twelve more years in school.* If, instead, I'd asked myself whether it was worth it to invest that time in becoming a doctor—a career I think would have been an interesting way to spend a decade—my choice would probably have been different. Even if I hadn't enjoyed a full ten years in the profession, my time in medical school wouldn't have been wasted. Time is only wasted by staying in a job you hate.

Thinking about your life in ten-year cycles also takes some pressure off the kind of Big Life Decisions that can paralyze people. It gives you the freedom to try things out without agonizing about whether you're making the right choice. There is no "the" about choices when life is long. You make *a* choice. If you're happy, great! If you're not, there's plenty of time to make a different choice.

Many of my friends tortured themselves about what major to choose in college. If I could talk to them now, I'd tell them, "Just pick one. After you graduate, work for five years, then pick another one." It's impossible to know in advance whether you're going to like the career you pick in college. The only way you'll know is to try it. If it's a terrible fit, you'll know within the first two years.

Even if it's a great fit for you now, the ten years between twenty and thirty are so transformative that you're not making a choice as the same person who'll experience the outcomes. You might love it for five years and get sick of it. When life is long, the only wrong choice is the one you don't make to initiate the next turn of the reinvention cycle.

THE SECOND MINDSET SHIFT

I bet I can guess what you're thinking. You're thinking, *If I hop around like this from one thing to the next, how will I ever get good at anything? Won't my career path look like a series of starts and failures rather than success?*

I have two answers: "No" and "Who Cares?"

No. A resume that shows ten years in three fields isn't a patchwork. You will probably have moved up the ladder or specialized in those years, and a decade is plenty of time to achieve mastery. Working a forty-hour week, you'll hit Malcolm Gladwell's famous ten thousand hours before you're halfway through.

So what? Is the point of your life to look good on paper? Let's redefine what success means. To me, a successful life is an interesting one. When I'm eighty-five, I want to have enough money saved not to be a burden on anyone, but when I'm sitting around the dinner table at the old folks' home, what I most want is to have fantastic stories. Or, as Hunter S. Thompson put it, "Life should not be a journey to the grave with the intention of arriving safely in a pretty and well-preserved body, but rather to skid in broadside in a cloud of smoke, thoroughly used up, totally worn out, and loudly proclaiming 'Wow! What a Ride!'"[17]

---

17 Hunter S. Thompson, *The Proud Highway: Saga of a Desperate Southern Gentleman, 1955-1967 (The Fear and Loathing Letters, Volume One)*, ed. Douglas Brinkley (New York: Ballantine Books, 1997).

LIFE IS LONG BUT NOT ENDLESS

You've probably heard that nobody lies on their deathbed wishing they'd spent more time at the office. I'm not sure that's true. I'd bet no artist ever died thinking *I wish I'd made less art.* When you love what you're doing—whether it's something new and fresh or just inherently interesting to you, time spent working isn't something you're going to regret when it runs out. Do you know what people *do* regret? The most common regret (according to Bronnie Ware, a palliative care nurse who worked with patients in the last twelve weeks of their lives) was having lived the life others expected of them rather than one that was true to themselves.[18]

Ware's patients mostly blamed a lack of courage (and if that's you, we'll tackle it in the next chapter), but I wonder how many simply bought into the idea that once you start a career, you have to stay in it until you die. Ware was working with people who'd mostly been born in the first half of the twentieth century, when few people got college degrees, so most of her patients had probably entered the workforce closer to eighteen than twenty-two. At that age, it's unsurprising that your first job would be whatever was expected of you. That young, there's hardly a true self to be true to, but by the time you've put five years into your first job, you should have a clear enough sense of what would be exciting to you to start planning your first reinvention cycle.

To me, living an interesting life and having fun doing it are enough reasons to reinvent yourself, but they aren't the only ones. Reinventing yourself is protective on two fronts—economic and emotional. Additionally, it's a gift to the people in your life; it's real self-care; it's lucky; and it's interesting to you, to your friends, and to researchers.

---

18 Bronnie Ware, *The Top Five Regrets of the Dying: A Life Transformed by the Dearly Departing* (Bloomington, IN: Balboa Press, 2011).

REINVENTION PROTECTS YOUR INCOME-EARNING OPTIONS

We looked at how quickly the world changes as proof that life is long, but it's also an excellent reason to think of your career as a series of ten-year cycles. If you were a manager in one of Blockbuster's nine thousand stores in 2004, you wouldn't have had much choice about reinventing your career well before your ten years were up. (There were only six hundred stores left open by 2011.)

Many workers find the only way to advance is by jumping ship, and why wouldn't they? Few public-sector companies today seem to feel much loyalty toward their employees or expect to keep people for their entire careers. Very few offer retention incentives like pensions or stock options. In fact, many organizations are shifting in the opposite direction—toward independent contractors to whom they aren't required to offer the minimum wage, overtime pay, unemployment insurance, paid sick days, family leave, workers' comp, or protections for health and safety or against discrimination and harassment.

One of the beauties of being in a cycle rather than on a path is that cycles overlap, and paths don't. It would be hard to hike the Appalachian Trail and the Grand Canyon at the same time, but in spring, many days still feel like winter, while others are indistinguishable from summer. When you look at your professional life as a continuing series of cycles, you almost always have something in your back pocket if your business model all but evaporates over five years.

REINVENTION PROTECTS YOU FROM YOURSELF

I kept working as an anesthetist while I ramped up my TV career, and my wild adventures over the weekends were a popular topic of conversation with the rest of the team. (Everybody else was as bored in that job as I was.) One day, having finished a story about oil miners in Kentucky, I mentioned that I was planning to quit anesthesia eventually and work full-time in TV. "Well, that's just irresponsible," the doctor said. "You can't change everything because you're not happy doing your job."

We'll put aside the professional and gender reasons he felt free to offer his unsolicited opinion on my career plans, and focus instead on the fact that I'd seen this guy put away five scotch and sodas in an evening. He was drinking himself to death, but I was irresponsible for wanting to change my life? We were both responding to job dissatisfaction in our own ways, but because his was incremental and didn't actually change anything, I doubt he even noticed the parallel. On the other hand, mine wasn't going to kill me.

Phase 0 is an emotionally dark time, and going too long between reinventions can make people self-destructive. Boredom and stagnant professional energy can turn into personal problems. Too often, people trying to relieve boredom or numb themselves to the discomfort caused by ignored warning signs turn to excessive drinking, eating, shopping, or risky sexual behavior.

One thing I've seen many women do when they're stuck in this phase is to focus all their dissatisfaction and boredom on their husbands or partners. The resulting divorce or breakup temporarily occupies their excess attention, and once that's done, they take on dating like a second full-time job. They fall in love and break up. They craft their online profiles and go on countless first dates. Dating is challenging and fun, exciting and scary enough that they can tolerate staying in a job that's none of those things.

I fell into this trap for a while, but for me, at least, it was a purely destructive force. I put dating on pause and focused on figuring out what was next for me professionally. I have a lot of empathy for women who stay stuck there, but Pamela Anderson (of all people) gave me the insight that career reinvention can be the way out for people who've been trapped in a bad dating loop a lot longer than I was.

At fifty-four with no musical theater experience, Anderson was approached by Broadway producers to take on the lead role in *Chicago*. I'm sure she knew it was what the reviewers would later call "stunt casting," but bless her if she didn't throw herself into the work! She got intensive singing and dancing coaching and ended up garnering nearly universal positive reviews. Before the show even opened, she was already reaping the psychological benefits of taking on something new professionally or, as she put it talking to *Vogue* magazine, "Thirty years of therapy or just one Broadway show, then I'll be fine."[19]

At the end of the documentary about her journey from screen to stage, Anderson says she's never been happier and that the only thing that could ruin things now would be a man. Friends, don't give up your whole life for a romantic partner. No one person, no matter how special, can bring you all the fulfillment in life you need. And it puts too much pressure on the relationship to expect them to try.

REINVENTION IS A GIFT TO OTHERS

This may come as a shock, but being bored and uninspired doesn't make you great to be around. Even if it doesn't drive you to pick fights with people over eucalyptus, that little cloud of negative

19   Lauren Valenti, "'I've Been Rehearsing My Whole Life for This': Pamela Anderson on Her Broadway Debut, TikTok's Obsession With Her Style, and Finally Setting the Record Straight," *Vogue*, March 22, 2022, https://www.vogue.com/article/pamela-anderson-broadway-debut-chicago.

energy that trails you home becomes part of the atmosphere there. Elsa wasn't a mean person. She loved her kids and spent hours every day driving them around and doing their laundry. But she was miserable and inadvertently spread that misery around. When you're bored, you'll look for something—anything—to create excitement in your life, and finding fault with others is one of the easiest ways to do it. So even if you're worried it might be selfish to get on the reinvention cycle, and can't do it for your own sake, do it for the sake of everyone else who spends time with you.

REINVENTION IS REAL SELF-CARE

Imagine it's Saturday morning, and you have no external obligations. Suddenly, you see me appear, dressed up like some older, female, Asian version of Morpheus from *The Matrix* with his red and blue pills. Take the blue pill, and you'll be whisked off to the spa. You'll spend the whole day soaking in warm water, getting a massage, and meditating. You won't put on shoes all day. There will be eucalyptus in your sauna.

The red pill takes you to the library. You'll research new careers and find one that feels like an exact fit. You'd be great at it. It pays well. You'll learn about the qualifications it takes and the different ways of adding them to your skillset. Maybe it's something you wanted to do when you were a kid but were talked out of it. Maybe it's the germ of an idea for a new business you can start building as a side hustle. Maybe it's a job you didn't know existed that combines your favorite school subject with your favorite kind of people.

How do you think you'd feel at the end of a blue-pill day? How about the red-pill one?

If I offered you the choice right now, which pill would you take?

Probably the blue one. Me too, if I'm honest. But if I showed up the next morning and the next? Assuming you don't just kick me out of your bedroom, I'm guessing that after a few weeks of taking the blue pill and doing self-care and relaxation, you'd start to feel sluggish and bored.

Taking the red pill and spending energy dreaming and researching possibilities for your life can be energizing, especially since it holds out a promise of an exciting future.

It's a quirk of the human brain, but we enjoy anticipation more than we like having the thing we anticipate. Having something up ahead that you're looking forward to is one of the best feelings around. When you think of your working life as a series of cycles, you always have something to look forward to. No matter how present you get meditating at the spa, we all naturally live in both the present and the future. When you expect the future to be a lot like the present, your mind slides easily across that timeline. When you expect the future to be a lot better than the present, it creates a little electric spark, and every time your mind hops tracks, it picks up energy. You have more energy in the present when you're excited about your future.

REINVENTION IS LUCKY

When people change their line of work every decade, they avoid the kinds of sameness that "exhaust the opportunities in their life," as Richard Wiseman, author of *The Luck Factor*, puts it. In contrast, the luckiest people he studied "went to considerable lengths to introduce variety and change into their lives."[20]

Did I get lucky with SnapNurse? Absolutely. I was ramp-

---

20 Richard Wiseman, *The Luck Factor: The Scientific Study of the Lucky Mind* (Bethesda, MD: Arrow Books, 2004), 4.

ing up a tech-powered healthcare staffing company (Uber for nurses) right before a global pandemic created a demand for nurses and forced changes in the law that made it even easier for me to do what I was attempting. But if I hadn't built that business as a side gig while doing my anesthesia job, that enormous opportunity would have skipped right over me. You're not going to get struck by lightning living in the basement. Regular reinvention means you're out there in a treeless field when a storm blows in. You create your luck.

REINVENTION IS INTERESTING

No matter where you are in the reinvention cycle, you'll have something exciting to think about when you're waiting at the DMV, or in the shower. You'll have a new topic of conversation each time you meet a friend for coffee or have dinner with your family. I came to this realization on my own and preached it to my friends. It's how I lured Elsa (and several other friends) out of retirement and into their own reinventions, so I knew it was true when I set out to write a book about it. What I didn't know was that it's backed by research.

INTERESTING IS SUCCESSFUL

By the time I realized life was long, I was making plenty of money and had already gone through two invention cycles. If I'd been able to follow my own future advice, I would have started sooner to look for what might come next, but it wasn't until my fourth decade that I realized how long a decade really is and how many I had left. I had chased success, caught it, and found it unfulfilling, so I changed my metric for a good life from "successful" to "interesting." And I ended up with both!

It's important not to set up interesting and successful as mutually exclusive—they're not. SnapNurse was massively successful, but I started it because I was looking for the next interesting thing. In fact, I think that's part of why it was successful. I'd argue that interesting is better than successful *and* that interesting leads to success.

When people do or study things that are interesting to them, it creates energy and focus. Procrastination disappears. Prioritization is easy. Self-discipline is required only to stop working long enough to maintain your most important relationship and get mundane tasks off your list. You throw yourself into the work, which becomes a kind of positive obsession, and that intensity breeds success.

I firmly believe human beings are obsessive by nature. Watch a baby watching anything. They're totally absorbed, soaking up all the information they can. Little kids are the same, obsessed with dinosaurs, princesses, horses, or trains. Then they hit school, where they're expected to pay attention to things that don't interest them, and the boredom conditioning begins.

My son was completely obsessed with Transformers when he was little. He still is. His interest was so focused and his knowledge so extensive that it helped get him into the selective art and design college that offers the country's only bachelor's degree in toy design. Can you imagine how he'll do when he graduates and goes to interview at Hasbro? He loves Transformers so much, and they're so interesting to him that success is going to come easily, and he'll never have trouble putting the work in because it won't feel like work.

I had the same experience in TV. What I was doing was so interesting that I worked long hours happily, picking up information everywhere, and self-assigned ongoing education to learn new skills. And my interest in the work made me successful in record time! I hadn't gone to film school; I didn't live in New York or have industry contacts. I didn't even have a media background, but the energy that my interest supplied put me ahead of other people who might have been more qualified but weren't as interested.

When you find something that fascinates you, you'll immerse yourself in it and dedicate hours to it. It won't feel like work, but it's almost guaranteed to lead to eventual success. Even if it doesn't, in the worst-case scenario, you will still have spent some portion of your life doing something interesting and having fun.

CHAPTER SUMMARY

Life is long. Because we can reasonably expect to live and work for decades, it doesn't make sense to see your first career choice as a lifetime commitment. Changing your mindset to think of your work life as a series of ten-year cycles has multiple benefits. It protects your income-earning options from a changing economic landscape and your psyche from the pain of being stuck or bored. It will make you happier and more engaged, which has downstream benefits for the people in your life and is the best form of self-care. It also increases your luck by exposing you to new opportunities and makes life more interesting. This, I believe, is a better goal than success. It's easier to plan for an interesting life and more likely to deliver both interesting and successful than aiming directly at success.

It's easier, but people still get stuck. In the next chapter, we'll dive into why.

Chapter 4

WHAT'S STOPPING YOU?

DURING MY TIME IN GRAD SCHOOL, REINVENTING MYSELF from schoolteacher and social worker to anesthetist, I met two other women in the same program, and we became great friends. We went to work in different Atlanta hospitals when we graduated, but we stayed close and met for dinner one Friday a month.

At about the four-year mark out of school, I noticed that our dinner conversations were getting steadily less fun. Rather than three excited young women swapping stories about what we'd learned, how much fun we were having, and *Oh my God, can you believe what we're getting paid!* we were starting to complain. We'd agreed that the work was getting boring, but two of us had had children already, and the third was pregnant.

At work one Thursday a year later, I was sitting on the stool where I would spend the next four hours watching the lines and bleeps that tracked a patient's vitals during surgery. I looked out the OR door to see if the doctor was on his way and saw the foot of a stretcher inch into view. It stopped. It lurched forward again. It stopped.

I watched, fascinated by its weird progression across the cross-section of the hallway visible through the open door. There was the patient's torso. There was a single hand on the stretcher frame. Then the nurse anesthetist came into view. She was probably in her late fifties but looked seventy. She had her right hand clamped on to the stretcher and her left on a walker. She'd push the stretcher forward, stop, drag the walker up, steady herself on it, and give the stretcher another push. *Oh Lord,* I thought. *That's going to be me one day if I don't get out soon!*

I told my friends that story at our next dinner, and we all agreed. We could not—would not—do this job forever. We didn't want to be old, in terrible health, and still doing the physically hard work of anesthesia. But even then, we recognized how hard it would be to leave. The pay was great. We all had kids. None of us could quit any time soon. I still remember the almost desperate look in my friends' eyes. We made a pact. We gave ourselves ten years. We all agreed we weren't going to do anesthesia any longer than a total of ten years. That meant we'd all be doing something else in five more years.

Five years later, we were all still doing anesthesia and meeting once a month for dinner. The only thing that had changed was the amount of wine. "Okay," I said. "It's been ten years. Time's up. What are we going to do next?"

They all agreed that now wasn't the right time. None of them could quit their jobs. Neither could I. I couldn't do what I'd done before and enroll in two years of full-time education to reinvent myself. But I was *not* going to do anesthesia for the rest of my life. I just wasn't. So, I went back into Phase 1 on the weekends. I started asking myself questions about what I wanted to do, what I could maybe do part-time, and what I could do that would be fun. Could my friends have done the same thing? Of course! But something was stopping them.

WHAT'S STOPPING YOU?

There are really only two possibilities. One's an old joke, and the other is fear. In this chapter, I'll tell you the joke and—with apologies to E.B. White, who compared explaining a joke to dissecting a frog (you will learn how it works, but it won't survive)—I'll talk through how it illustrates one of the things that keeps people stuck. I'll then catalog the different garden-variety fears that can keep people from living their most interesting lives and take a look at three special cases—the sunk-cost fallacy, social conditioning, and the damage done by trauma—and offer some ways to defeat them.

AN OLD JOKE

An old man is sitting on his front porch with a dog next to him. The dog is pitiful—almost as old as the man, with a gray muzzle and huge soulful eyes. A young guy, passing by, hears the poor thing whimpering and walks up to the porch. "What's wrong with your dog?" he asks.

"He's sittin' on a nail."

"Really?"

"Yup."

"Why doesn't he move?"

"I reckon it don't hurt enough yet."

If you haven't hit the rock bottom of your emotional journey, this may be what's stopping you. Change is hard. There's no doubt about it. It's easier to stay where you are, where everything's familiar, sitting on your nail. This is why there are so many motivational posters about getting out of your comfort zone. Comfort (and even tolerable discomfort) can be very hard to leave behind.

If the inertia of comfort is what's keeping you stuck, you can deliberately increase the pain of staying put. I'm not suggesting you go sit on nails. Instead, you can use the very same part of your brain that's keeping you from launching into your next reinvention cycle—your imagination.

Instead of imagining how hard it will be to change, imagine what will happen if you don't. When I was still sitting on my nail as an anesthetist, my imagination got an assist from real life in the form of the nurse anesthetist with her walker. I leveraged my fear of one thing to overcome my fear of something else.

So go nuts! Imagine the worst-case future of your current path. Make it one-handed-walker bad. If you feel stuck, bored, irritable, and unmotivated now, how much worse will you feel after ten more years of the same? Really picture it. Now add failing eyesight and stiffening joints to your picture.

Feeling more motivated now?

If comfort isn't stopping you, the other possibility is fear. (There are a few others—the sunk-cost fallacy, social conditioning, and trauma—but even they are reducible to a fear of loss, a fear of breaking social norms, and the residual fear of having survived something life-threatening. We'll look at each of these three fear subvariants at the end of the chapter, but let's tackle the biggie first.)

A POISON BOUQUET

Fear comes in as many varieties as flowers, and each of us picks our own unique selection and arranges it differently. I could write a whole book about fear—other people have—but I'm honestly not all that interested. To me, the point of fear is to drive change. Conversely, if you're not changing even though you want to, fear is probably the reason, so let's identify the four most common fear flowers and weed them out.

FEAR OF LOSS

I remember having lunch with a friend of mine, Kristie, who absolutely hated her job. She hated the commute, the company, the people she worked with, and the work itself. "So why don't you leave?" I asked her.

"They pay me too much."

When good money is a bad thing, fear of loss is what's holding you back. Kristie was married to a guy who made as much as she did, and they had more than enough saved to keep living in comfort, even if it took her five years to get back to earning a comparable salary. I pointed this out to her and added, "And who knows? You might make even more in a new job doing something that really energizes you."

Kristie admitted that was not just possible but likely, and for a moment, she looked a little lost. "But they have a great retirement plan!" she said triumphantly.

"You're forty."

"Yeah?"

"You're going to work another twenty-five years hating nine hours out of every weekday for a retirement plan?"

Kristie's face went blank. Then she burst out laughing. She leaned across the table conspiratorially. "You know what's extra crazy?" she whispered. "I honestly don't think the company will make it that long. They're going to go bust, and then—poof! No retirement plan!"

"Well, good thing you're sacrificing so much for it then," I said, and we ordered another round of drinks.

Kristie thought she was trapped in golden handcuffs, but here's the thing: gold is soft. It's so soft that even Tiffany's $55,000 all-gold necklace is 18 karat and not pure 24 karat gold. When you think you can't "leave it all" to take a risk on something better, remember it's a fake. It's thinking left over from the "your career is a path" mindset.

In the career reinvention cycle, you don't leave anything when you start something new. You phase the new thing in and then phase the old one out. If fear of loss is keeping you stuck, reassure yourself. You can wear those shiny handcuffs as long as you need them.

FEAR OF FAILURE

I have a friend, Michele, who's written most of six books. She starts them, works hard on them, and then, before she gets to the end, starts another one. She's afraid that if she finishes a book, she won't have a good reason not to publish it. What if she puts it out in the world and people don't like it? She's afraid no one will buy it—or worse, they'll buy it and read it and leave a bad review.

I have a little game I like to play called "What's the worst that could happen?" I'd guess how you play is pretty obvious. I played it with Michele, and her absolute worst-case scenario wasn't going bankrupt and having to live under a bridge; it was a one-star review. She was embarrassed by that, but I get it. (I get it even more now that I'm writing a book myself!)

Michele wasn't afraid she'd write a bad book. She wasn't afraid the book would fail. She was afraid of how a bad review would make her feel. She wasn't sure she could handle that feeling. Her fear of failure was actually a fear of shame. I see the same thing in entrepreneurs. They can bounce back easily when their startup goes down in flames but only if they can tell themselves a story that keeps shame out of the narrative.

The fear of failure is often bolstered by the statistics that sadistic people love to share. *Did you know half of all marriages end in divorce? Did you know half of all new businesses fail?* These data points aren't wrong, but they won't do you any favors, so I recommend ignoring them to the extent that you can. If you don't believe you'll beat the odds, you won't try. Sure, only 2 percent of female entrepreneurs get funded by private equity and venture capital, but that's not the same as zero. Someone is getting that money, and that someone could be you. Even if it isn't, I built SnapNurse to $1 billion in revenue without any private equity. There are ways around every statistic.

Here's a statistic to keep at the front of your mind: you'll fail at 100 percent of the things you don't try.

Of course, the easiest way to deal with the fear of failure is to make failure impossible. You do that by defining success on your own terms. If success means critical or financial success, fear may win, especially if your sense of self is fragile or particularly vulnerable to shame. If success means learning something about an industry, meeting new people, and having fun, you can't lose. All the metrics for victory are within your control, so choose to play the game you can win.

Another of our cultural myths contributes to our fear of failure—the "happily ever after" ending. It's the same kind of thinking that calls a twenty-year marriage that ends in divorce a failed marriage. A reinvention isn't a failure if you've had a good run and then choose to do something else. Ziggy Stardust didn't fail. Bowie just got bored and moved on.

If you look at your career as a single path, a static, straight line rather than a dynamic cycle, modest success looks like a plateau. You move up the ladder when you're young, reach your max level of performance, and stabilize. If you're ambitious, the only victory condition is a continual rise, success following success.

When you expect your career to cycle, you can reach the end of a winning streak without losing. After the board of Snap-Nurse replaced me as CEO, I'll confess I had a day or two where I let it ruin my mood. But then I gave myself a talking-to. When I started the company, my goal wasn't to be its lifetime CEO. I exited with an excellent track record, winning Inc 5000's second-fastest-growing company (and first-fastest in healthcare), and I left at its peak with a tidy sum of money. That's not failure. It was, in fact, an excellent run. I was burned out. I had gained fifty pounds, had high blood pressure, and was prediabetic and out of shape. I didn't even recognize myself in my award pictures! I'm grateful for a board that found a new CEO with the vigor and energy to take SnapNurse to the next level while I got back to the gym, lost the fifty pounds, and brought my blood sugar under control. Today, I feel better than ever and ready to tackle my next reinvention!

Expecting things to get progressively better or never end is a guarantee of failure. Nothing lasts forever, and when you're at the end of something, the question isn't *Did I fail?* but *Did I have a good run?* Honestly, I'd call anything a win if you get out with your life and a few good stories.

FEAR OF CHANGE

Hamlet nailed this one with his "rather bear those ills we have than fly to others that we know not of." Our innate distrust of the unknown is the reason evolution ended up selecting for boredom. Without it, our ancestors would probably never have left the caves they were born in.

Every animal on the planet is wary of the unfamiliar. That

makes sense. If you're alive, it means that nothing in the status quo has killed you. That's automatically more than you know about anything new. There's absolutely nothing wrong with this, and people who are happy with the status quo should stay there. It's only when you aren't happy with how things are that the fear of change becomes a hindrance.

Stealth is the best way to deal with the fear of change. Think of it as a mental watchdog that will sleep peacefully when nothing is going on, only perks up his ears when you walk through the room, but freaks out if a stranger enters.

Make very small changes to keep your fear of change from going on alert. It's the same tactic you use on children when they (for equally sound evolutionary reasons) refuse to try a new food. How do they know it won't kill them? *Just try a tiny bite.* In Chapter 6, I'll talk more about defining these little job nibbles, but the important thing to know now is that the fear of change never goes away. But it's a very primitive fear and one you can learn to outwit.

FEAR OF JUDGMENT

I'm not going to lie to you. Yes, some people will judge you if you try something new. But hey, some people are probably out there judging you for what you're doing now. You really can't please everyone all the time. Michele's agonized "What if they hate my book?" is one way this fear shows up. Another friend of mine used to be in a band, and every night, on the way to the venue, the bassist would say, "No one will show up."

And the drummer would agree, "And thousands will hate us."

Who is this all-powerful *they* whose opinion we're so worried about? Is it your friends and family? Probably not. Of course, they're afraid of change just like you are, so it's possible that the changes you make will frighten them, and they won't handle it well. But if you can recognize that for what it is and reassure them that leaving your old life doesn't mean leaving them, they'll probably settle down.

So, if the people you care about aren't *they*, why do you care what *they* think? Are you going to give your anxious assumptions of what some nameless, faceless *they* think that kind of power over you? I didn't think so!

Of course, sometimes, one of *them* shows up at a Christmas party and tells you to your face what they think, but I'd be willing to bet that they're not out there living their best life. In these situations, ask yourself, *Would I trade lives with this person?* Remember, this is a person with enough lack of social skills to say something like that to a relative stranger in the first place.

There's also some truth to the old "the tallest poppies get cut" idea. There's something about the dark side of human nature that makes certain kinds of people go after successful people just because they're successful. It's even an established syndrome called, you guessed it, "tall poppy syndrome."[21]

Sometimes, the judgment you're afraid of that's keeping you stuck is harder to dismiss or deflect. If the thing you want to leave behind is something that other people are invested in emotionally or financially, they may well be hurt or disappointed by your new plans.

If your parents have a lot of their self-worth and pride tied up in your "successful" career, the fact that it's making you miserable may not seem like a good enough reason to them for quitting. If they just spent a few hundred grand on your education, and

---

21 Sonia Blair, "Breaking Down Tall Poppy Syndrome," *Harper's Bazaar*, n.d., https://harpersbazaar.com.au/tall-poppy-syndrome-wellbeing-mental-health/.

after a year, you no longer want to be a lawyer, they're probably not going to be pleased.

I can just imagine how the conversation went when the actor and comedian Ken Jeong told his Korean parents he didn't want to be a doctor anymore. Which is why I'm betting he didn't. In fact, I just checked, and as of April 2023, he's still a licensed physician in California. But his parents probably know about the acting by now.

When I first started thinking that working in TV might be fun and learning about how I could break into it, I didn't tell anyone. Even after I'd sold a couple of shows, I kept the news mostly to myself.

Especially in Phase 1, I'd recommend this stealth tactic. As excited as you are about your reinvention, and as much as you might be bubbling over with all the interesting things you're learning about this next big adventure, the cycle is delicate here. One harsh reaction or critical comment that would bounce off you once you've had a few successes in your new venture can puncture you early on. New ideas need your protection.

THE SUNK-COST FALLACY

Even though I think this is just fear of loss in disguise, it's worth unmasking because I've seen it keep otherwise perceptive people from going into the next phase of their reinvention. In economics, a sunk cost is simply one you can't get back. In real life, it looks like spending more to repair your car than it's worth because you've already spent so much on it. In a stalled reinvention cycle, it sounds like "I can't leave! I've dedicated so much time (or money or education) to getting where I am."

You're not getting those hours or dollars back, but you do get to take everything you learned with you. This is the excuse (and it *is* an excuse) that I heard most from my friends who were anesthetists and hated their jobs as much as I hated mine. Even the ones who weren't bothered by leaving the steady paycheck felt like they couldn't quit because they'd already put so much time into the job. This is the same kind of thinking that keeps people chucking coins into slot machines. They can't quit now! Not when they're down. Surely, they're due for a win.

If you feel like you can't start a new cycle because you've already invested so much in the last one, let me ask you this: would you sell your happiness for it? If I had the magical ability to bestow happiness upon you, would you trade me your law degree for it? I think I'd sell pretty much anything but my children.

Everything you've done up to now has gotten you where you are. It was worth doing just to arrive at a place where you have choices to make about what to do with your next ten or twenty years. And here's the real kicker: you get to take all of it with you.

After college, I "wasted" my education by waiting tables and working for two years at the Sheepfold homeless shelter for battered women and children. If I'd stayed, I could probably have moved up the ranks and become a manager or leveraged my experience into a job at a larger nonprofit. When I left, I "threw away" all that. But was it wasted? Nope!

Years later, it got me into the Emory University School of Medicine's Anesthesia program.

My "wasted" college education also allowed me to get a job as a science teacher two years after I graduated. Two more years later, I decided to attend medical school. Applying required me to take the MCAT—an arduous eight-hour-long exam for which people usually take months to study. I didn't have months. I took it without much preparation and did quite well. Why? It wasn't the college courses I'd taken so many years ago. The years

I'd "wasted" teaching AP Biology, Chemistry, and Physics had prepared me beautifully.

Sitting in the entrance interview for Emory—one of the best schools in the country for what I wanted to do—the old, white, male doctor looked up from my application. "Well, your MCAT scores are fine, but you know, your grades aren't that great."

I just nodded. I knew.

He gave me a searching look. "Still, I think we'll go ahead and admit you. Emory is committed to training people who genuinely care about others, and I see you worked at a homeless shelter for two years."

I'm not the only one with this kind of story. Steve Jobs didn't even graduate from college, but the years he "wasted" on the Reed campus included a calligraphy class (which might seem like a timewaster even if he'd ended up with a degree). But he credits that class with the priority he later put on ensuring the first Mac supported a wide variety of fonts—a feature that distinguished it from its more established rivals (and eventually led to the fabled "font war" with Microsoft).

SOCIAL CONDITIONING

If the idea that life is long seems strange, it's not your fault. We've all been conditioned to think that it's short, and I don't think that's just because it used to be. Our culture is obsessed with youth and so terrified of getting older that the anti-aging market was estimated at over $60 billion worldwide in 2021.[22]

22 "Value of the Global Anti-Aging Market 2021–2027," published by Dominique Petruzzi, September 26, 2023, Statista, https://www.statista.com/statistics/509679/ value-of-the-global-anti-aging-market/#statisticContainer.

It's why thirty-three seemed prohibitively old to me when I was considering med school.

"Life is short" and "time flies" are clichés people constantly repeat, and I don't think there's a mother out there who hasn't been instructed to enjoy every moment of her child's infancy because it goes by so fast. Nobody tells kids, "You have plenty of time." Nobody tells fifty-year-olds that either, but it's still true. Nobody does the math! Life is barely half-over at fifty.

My friend with the six unfinished books thinks she's too old to start a writing career, but Laura Ingalls Wilder published the first of her eight-book *Little House* series when she was sixty-five. (And that was in 1932, when the life expectancy for women was sixty-three-and-a-half!) I started SnapNurse when I was forty-nine, but I've talked to plenty of women in their thirties who thought they were too old to start a new business, even though there's solid research that says startups with older founders do better.

Our cultural narrative is still "life ends at forty," and only poor people work multiple jobs. While it's certainly true that the insultingly low minimum wage and cost of living in the US mean it's almost impossible to support a family on forty hours a week at fourteen dollars an hour, there's no reason why we must buy into the idea that a single-track career path is the only good option.

If you're making six figures but hate your job, nobody's going to suggest you take a part-time gig to build up your skills doing something you might love and be able to transition to later on. It probably won't even occur to you to take night school classes to pick up the skills you'd need to go into the dream career you gave up on when you were younger. Have you ever known anyone over thirty who used their Saturdays and Sundays to study for the LSAT because they always wanted to be a lawyer? Me neither.

I think we're also conditioned to believe the single-track, one-career-for-life narrative by the way our educational system is structured. Even though it's widely known that it was set up to train children to be factory workers, we still indoctrinate kids into a *Groundhog Day* routine starting when they're five.

They go to the same building and take the same subjects with the same kids and the same teachers, day after day, year after year. If they're lucky, there's some variation between their Tuesdays and Thursdays and their Mondays, Wednesdays, and Fridays, and at least they get summers off, but the pattern of working roughly eight hours a day every weekday and doing the same thing for years is well baked into us by the time we're eighteen, and it continues whether we go to college or into the workforce.

Then social conditioning about being a "responsible adult" takes over. Being a responsible adult means you stay in a stable job. You don't take a pay cut to try something new. You don't go off on adventures anymore. Excitement is something for young people. Your job is to be boring now that you're "old." This social conditioning gets compounded if you're a woman or when you have children. Your job now is to be safe for children, put their needs ahead of your own, and take no risks at all.

TRAUMA

Trauma causes a fear different from the other fears we've discussed that can stop people from living in a ten-year reinvention cycle. Adverse childhood experiences (which social psychologists call ACEs) can cause serious and long-lasting developmental, psychological, and physical health problems.

The women I worked with at the Sheepfold had enough work dealing with the repercussions of their abuse that they were already doing the equivalent of working two jobs. People who were abused, neglected, or raised in dysfunctional homes, like I was, are going to have a job to do reinventing their worldview and coping strategies before they can start reinventing their professional lives.

Of course, none of us escape childhood unscathed, so it's perfectly possible that even with just one or no ACEs, you can find your childhood scars stopping you or keeping you stuck. Either way, two things can help: getting a life mentor and reframing your past as proof of your indomitability.

Life Mentors

I say "life mentor" to make a distinction between the way we usually use the word "mentor" and the way we'll use it here. A mentor helps you learn and advance professionally. Life mentors help you learn and improve how you manage life.

I grew up with a mentally ill mother and a father who left the country, taking my younger brother with him. That experience and the ones that stemmed from it—having to care for my mother and support myself—left me with a great deal of unprocessed pain, emotional blockages, and some very bad examples.

I was very fortunate to find a life mentor in the woman from whom I rented a bedroom after college. Tooti was my friend Julie's mom and an incredible mother. She was also a psychiatric nurse. She taught me how to deal with my painful emotions and gave me a model of a healthy family. Her whole family loved each other and had Christmases with a tree, presents, and people who came over to the house with "white elephant" gifts. It showed me that my future didn't have to repeat my past and that I could choose to make my own future family more like theirs than the one I'd grown up with. To this day, Christmas is a big deal at my house as I model for my kids what I learned from Tooti and her husband, Dave.

A traumatic past can get in the way of your future. It can stop you and keep you stuck. But it doesn't have to. Having a life mentor makes a huge difference.

Reframing Your Past

If you're from the inner city, or you're a single mom, or you come from nothing, and you're still sitting there reading a book about reinventing your life, stop for a moment and look at everything you've already overcome to get to this point. You should have more confidence for having beaten the odds than anyone who never faced a deck stacked against them.

You already know you're resilient. You've already racked up years of survival training. Confidence builds like stacking blocks, and you already have a solid foundation. Your emotional scars may make you doubt it, but it's there, and if you can clear away some of the wreckage with the help of a life mentor or therapist, I'll bet you'll find the basis for a lifetime of steadily more exciting, more rewarding reinventions.

THE ANTIDOTE

At the start of this chapter, I said that there were only two answers to its titular question: *What's stopping you?* If comfortable inertia was keeping you stuck, I recommended frightening yourself. If fear is what's keeping you stuck, everyone knows the antidote, right? The answer to fear is courage. You need to feel the fear and do it anyway. But to my mind, that's a bit of a circular argument.

What do I need to stop being stopped by fear?
Courage.

What's courage?

The unwillingness to be stopped by fear.

Great. Thanks. So not helpful.

Once again, a circle is more effective than a straight line. Rather than trying to run right at your fears and wrestle them into submission, I recommend setting courage aside and working on confidence. Confidence is simply the belief that you can do something. It's not even the belief that you can defeat fear. It's the belief that you can do *something*. Anything. And that's what lets you tiptoe around fear rather than tackling it head-on. But even that takes some courage.

CHAPTER SUMMARY

Comfortable inertia and fear are the two primary reasons people get stuck and don't reinvent themselves. Vividly imagining the future that's most likely if nothing changes works well to motivate you to overcome inertia while learning to recognize the different faces of fear can help you know how to confront it.

If you're afraid of losing the money and benefits that go with staying stuck in a job you no longer enjoy, the gradual phasing into and out of cycles can help you move forward without fear.

Work on defining success on your own terms to shut down the fear of failure that's often the fear of shame. Expect reinventions to end, not last forever. The primal fear of change can be tricked by making small, gradual changes. Recognizing that the "they" who are doing the judging are often not the people who matter can help you get over the fear of judgment.

For fear's first two special cases, the same truth pertains: identifying the fear unmasks it and strips it of much of its power. The sunk-cost fallacy is a fallacy, and social conditioning is conditional. Healing may be necessary to address the lingering fear caused by trauma, but getting a life mentor and reframing past challenges as proof of resilience can help.

Finally, focus on building confidence over courage. In the next chapter, we'll go deeper into the relationship between the two and how to increase both.

Chapter 5

COURAGE AND CONFIDENCE

I HAVE A FRIEND WHO'S IN HER MID-SIXTIES, AND although, thankfully, there's no Guinness World Record for such things, I'd bet she's been rejected by more men in the last thirty years than anyone else on earth. She's on a cycle of her own—she meets someone new, he's wonderful, there's a month of giddy joy, then heartbreak. Then she meets someone new. Now that's what I call courage!

Career failures and rejections can knock the air out of you, but I don't think there's an arena of greater vulnerability than dating, especially for women of "a certain age." And yet my friend went out on another first date yesterday.

I've certainly seen plenty of people—male and female— lose their courage in the face of disappointed love. Out of the understandable desire to protect their hearts, they stop offering them to people. They quit putting themselves "out there" where they're exposed to rejection.

COURAGE AND CONFIDENCE

At the end of the last chapter, I said that confidence is the belief that you can do something—anything. My friend has no confidence that her next date will be the first with her future husband, but she knows that she can look her best and show up for it. It's not an easy thing to do, but it is something she can control, even if she can't control the outcome. Going on dates builds her confidence in her ability to go on dates, and that gives her courage. In this chapter, we'll look at where courage comes from, where confidence goes, and how to get it back, create more, and protect it.

WHERE COURAGE COMES FROM

My friend is relentless. Her goal is to find someone to marry and love for the rest of her life. She wants it badly enough that at least once a month, she wills herself to dress up and go out on another first date. And she shows up for that date courageously, with optimism and enthusiasm—not for what's likely, but for what's possible. Her courage comes from two places: she wants to find love enough to risk almost certain disappointment, and she was raised to be brave. In other words, courage comes from desire. It's also shaped by the way we've been raised.

DESIRE

To a certain extent, the quality of a goal can be measured by how much failure or disappointment you're willing to endure in its pursuit. High-quality goals are the ones you want badly enough to still pursue even when they seem far away and hard to reach. In other words, high-quality goals give you courage.

I've seen people show amazing courage in the face of grueling infertility treatments because their desire to have a baby made them relentless. I believe the best way to tackle something big and frightening is by breaking it into manageable baby steps, but sometimes you will have to run right up the face of a brick wall, and when you do, only desire beats gravity.

CHILDHOOD

There seems to be a genetic component to courage. Some kids come into the world as brave adventurers, and others start out more timidly. I have a friend who has two girls, both raised the same way, and the first time she and her husband took the kids skiing, the younger was flying down a black diamond run by the end of the trip while the older was still inching along the bunny slope.

This kind of innate fearlessness can be problematic. A child with no natural caution may try dangerous things with the same lack of hesitation that my friend's daughter took to the slopes. It can be frightening for parents, and I'm proud of my friend for letting her try.

A parent can't give a child courage, but how you're raised certainly affects how brave you are by the time you leave home. Parents who are adventurous and teach their kids that failure is recoverable and that they are resilient will have children who are more courageous at eighteen than parents who don't encourage their kids to challenge themselves and try things.

I understand it's hard. Our first job as parents is to keep our kids safe, but I think our second job is not to make them too safe. We can do that best by modeling courage ourselves.

It was important to me to raise brave kids, so I always shared my adventures with them. They grew up seeing me take risks, and they shared in my wins. They even made me a little poster when the first TV show to list my name in the credits aired!

They saw how hard I worked, and they saw it pay off. They also saw that when it didn't, it didn't destroy me. When they were old enough, I roped them into the hard work too. They were teens in the early days of SnapNurse, and when the pandemic hit, they pitched in to do whatever I needed them to. My son was already in college in 2021 when I won Ernst and Young's National Entrepreneur of the Year, but I took my daughter to the awards ceremony, and she got to enjoy some of the rewards of the big risks I'd taken and the work we'd done together.

WHERE CONFIDENCE GOES

In the same way that confidence can be built up, it can also be whittled away. I've seen confident women lose faith in themselves after a string of professional setbacks or by staying too long in a bad marriage. Certainly, this is another place where the damage done by ACEs can show up. Kids who were raised with abuse or neglect may have learned early on that nothing they did could keep them safe.

On the other hand, my dad left me alone with my mentally ill mother when he went back to Korea, and as damaging as that was on other fronts, it forced me to get a job and start taking care of myself at fifteen. By the time I went to college, I had a confidence in my ability to live on my own away from home that none of my classmates had. Most of them weren't worried that they couldn't handle it and believed they'd be just fine without their parents nearby, but I *knew* I could because I already had.

Sexism can also be a drain. Confidence is a trait that seems to be encouraged in and expected of men, while women are often conditioned not to brag about themselves and to be more critical of our faults. But since you've already shaken off your social conditioning by starting to think of life as long, you can have confidence that you can do it again!

Finally, confidence can evaporate over time. One of the biggest dangers of the linear career path is that doing the same thing year after year slowly erodes your confidence in your ability to do new things. If it's been twenty years since you've picked up a new skill, you may doubt whether you can learn everything you'll need to know to switch careers.

You can.

But our brains do work against us here. We all have what psychologists call a negativity bias that causes us to remember failure and forget success. It's another mental characteristic that was useful to remember which of those berries made us sick, but now it just gets in our way. I'll bet you can remember word-for-word a time someone said something unkind or critical, but can you exactly quote anyone's praise? Probably not.

WHERE CONFIDENCE COMES FROM

The best and worst thing about confidence is that it's entirely self-generated. No matter how much your mom tells you you're great, if you haven't proven it to yourself, you're not going to believe it. On the other hand, even if everyone, including your mom, tells you that you can't do something, once you've done even a sliver of it, you'll know you can.

Whether you've never had much self-confidence or lost your belief in yourself after a series of setbacks, the way to build it up is to figure out the biggest small step you can take without waking up your internal watchdog. The easiest place to start is the past.

CONFIDENCE RECLAMATION

Pretty much everything you're doing right now except breathing is something you once didn't know how to do. While I probably can't convince you to feel good about the fact that you can now dress yourself, I am confident that there are plenty of other things you accomplished in your past that could give you a confidence boost if you took a minute to remember or reframe them.

WHAT HAVE YOU COMPLETED?

Think of everything you've finished. Over the course of your life, how many books have you read? How many courses have you taken? How many times have you done the Christmas shopping? How many job applications have you completed? How many times have you moved?

I'll bet you have a long history of finishing things that you've disregarded. If you lack confidence in your ability to finish things because there are a few you started and didn't complete, run the numbers. Every day, you finish more tasks than you have projects left undone.

WHAT HAVE YOU ACCOMPLISHED?

Have you raised kids, changed a tire, or kept yourself fed? Have you maintained a garden or kept a pet alive? What jobs have you done? How many errands have you run? How many friendships have you made? How many trips have you taken? How many times have you cleaned out your closet? How many times have you recovered from illness or injury (physical or emotional)?

We too often reserve a feeling of accomplishment for things we've done for the first time or when they were difficult or took years. This is silly. By deciding such a large percentage of your accomplishments don't count, you're not getting an accurate view of how much you're capable of doing.

What Have You Learned?

How many things like sports, cooking, or your current job have you gotten better at in the last five years? Improvement in anything means you learned how to get better at it. How many kinds of exercise have you tried? How many subjects did you pass in school? How many licenses do you have? What skills have you taught someone else (including your kids)? You know a lot more than you know you do. We'll talk about getting it all on your resume in the next chapter, but for now, just take a moment and feel good about it.

Positive Proof Positive

Regularly remind yourself of these stealth successes. This is the closest to the rah-rah positive thinking "every day in every way" philosophy that I can get. Power-posing and pep talks in the mirror won't work if you don't believe them. The only way to build confidence is to succeed, but it's all too easy to forget or discount past successes. Particularly when confidence is at a low ebb, it's tempting to believe you've never succeeded at anything. But that, my friend, is fear talking, trying to keep you small.

Your fear is lying to you.

Don't try to answer it by bluffing or puffing yourself up. Answer it with cold, hard, inarguable facts. You now have proof of positive traits and accomplishments. Remind yourself regularly of all you've completed, accomplished, and learned, and let the facts boost your confidence.

I'll bet you had to work hard to get wherever you are right now. If you could do that, you can do this.

Maybe the biggest confidence-sapping lie is the idea that education or experiences can be wasted. If you tried something and it didn't work out, that old "happily ever after" narrative can convince you that nothing good came out of it. In the same way that having taught science prepared me to pass the MCAT, even though I had no idea that was something I'd want to do one day, any experience you've had might come in handy in some unexpected way in the future. Nothing is wasted.

CONFIDENCE CREATION

You can reclaim confidence from the past, but the only way to build more is to do something you're not confident about. You earn your courage. The trick is to find something between "not confident" and "too scary." In Chapter 6, we'll talk about how to break the work of Phase 1 into manageable baby steps, but even before we get to that, you can start building your confidence in one of three ways.

Try Something New

Review your bucket list; think back to the school subjects, extracurricular activities, sports, hobbies, or games you used to love doing as a kid but haven't touched in twenty years; or google "fun things to do near me."

Find a class, meet-up group, or event that sparks a little glimmer of fear-tinged excitement in you, and make a reservation. Ideally, this exercise will introduce new people as well as a new activity, but if that puts it over the scary line, taking part in something new on your own is a legitimate first step.

If you already take a weekly salsa class, a tango class isn't going to cut it, but if you loved to dance as a kid and have no idea whether you can still move your body to music, many places will let you take the first class for free.

If you haven't spoken French since high school, you can probably find a conversational French meet-up in a local bistro, or you could attend a writers' accountability group if fear is keeping you from working on that novel.

Go Somewhere New

Take an overnight trip by yourself to another city. If that's too scary, make it a day trip. If you're confident you can do that, push it in the other direction. Go out of state or to another country. Figure out how far away you need to go to trigger a bit of anxiety about your ability to navigate there, then book your travel!

Make this an ongoing exercise, going a little further afield each time. Even if you need to start as close to home as going to a new restaurant alone, you could end up in Italy!

Think of this not just as confidence-building but also as adventure training wheels.

Remember what I said in the Introduction: success takes time, but interesting can start immediately. Go somewhere new enough that you'll come back with something interesting to talk about the next time you meet a friend for coffee. For bonus points, start that conversation with "What's the most interesting thing you did last week?"

Do Something Better

Pick one thing you've already planned to do next week—cooking for your kid's bake sale, going to the gym, or doing some aspect of your job. Make it something you've done before and are completely confident you will do. (If you already go to the gym every week, great, but if it's something you've been promising yourself to get back to, don't use it for this exercise.)

Think of five things you could do to make it better—either better for others or more fun for you. Spend the extra time to decorate those cupcakes, add a pound to your weight-lifting, or pedal your flat-out hardest at spin class. Find a way to make that PowerPoint deck funny or gamify emptying your inbox.

In an ideal world, there would be a little external validation in the form of a compliment on your cookies, a pound lost on the scale, or a laugh at your jokes, but even if there isn't, you'll know you've done something with excellence, and that will build your confidence.

CONFIDENCE PROTECTION

Considering how vital confidence is to your ability to initiate and move through the reinvention cycle and how much work you're doing to reclaim and create it, it's worth adding two things you can do to safeguard it from the world (and from that part of yourself that would rather not be so interesting, thank you very much).

Selective Blindness and Deafness

There is something perverse about human nature that makes people want to tell every engaged couple the story of the most catastrophic divorce they know of and every pregnant woman the most horrendous birth story they've ever heard. This instinct will also kick in for some people if you let them know you're trying anything new.

In the previous chapter, I recommended keeping your reinvention projects secret to avoid exposing yourself to judgment, but this human weirdness is less about judgment than a ghoulish glee some people take in their ability to frighten you.

When I decided my next reinvention cycle would be into the largely male-dominated world of entrepreneurship, it wasn't my friends but the world itself that "helped" me out this way. If you're a female entrepreneur, statistics aren't your friend. Only 2 percent of private equity funding goes to women. Ninety percent of all startups fail.

Coming across this kind of data can really undermine your confidence. It's so easy to think, *Why should I even try?* If you can't just unhear this kind of discouraging information, flip it on its ear. See only the two and the ten. No divorce is fun, and no birth is painless, but the horror stories people tell stand out as remarkable because they're outliers. In the same way, starting a new business is never easy. But look at the outliers here. It's not that *no* women get funded or that *all* startups fail. That 2 percent probably represents several hundred women. That 10 percent is thousands of businesses, and there's no reason why you can't be one of those hundreds and thousands.

Choose to take an optimistic stance. Who knows? Maybe five years from now, that 2 percent will be 20 because the women who won in the past are funding other women now. Be one of them. Some (admittedly small) percentage of women get funded, and many startups thrive. Focus on that.

Selective Change

A while back, a friend of mine built up the courage to leave a marriage in which she was consistently taken for granted and ignored. In the spirit of overcoming the inertia of her stale marriage, she also quit her job and joined SnapNurse. Newly single and in a new job, she had a bit of a nervous breakdown. It was too much too quickly.

Her life is radically different and significantly better now. She's financially secure and happily single, but she could have gotten there more gradually. You don't have to change everything all at once. In fact, I encourage you not to, even if you're feeling brave enough.

A TRICK AND A TEST

The final trick for finding courage is to want something badly enough that you don't mind being scared or don't notice when you've been knocked on your butt. As you go through the day-dreaming and desire-finding exercises in the next chapter, test those you come up with against the fears we've identified. If you can look straight at fear and know you're willing to risk it for the dream you've found and the future you want, you'll know you have one worthy of your reinvention.

CHAPTER SUMMARY

It's hard to just "be brave," but having seen, in the last chapter, all the ways that fear can stop us or keep us stuck, it's well worth your time to work on developing courage—not directly, but with the same kind of stealth that makes fear so powerful. Our childhoods may shape our innate courage, but a strong desire to reach an important goal can give us the courage to act in the face of fear.

Because confidence is built incrementally and can be eroded by setbacks or sexism, it's important to reclaim it by remembering past accomplishments, to create more of it by taking risks that are small enough to get past your fears, and to protect it by focusing on success stories. With desire-driven courage and incremental confidence, you can reinvent fearlessly. The first step is to figure out what you want enough to make you brave.

Chapter 6

PHASE 1, DISCOVERY

THE WORK OF PHASE 1 IS TO DISCOVER WHAT YOU WANT
and explore how you might get it. Sometimes, you know right
away. Maybe there's a dream you deferred that still haunts your
thoughts. Maybe you picked up this book because you just discovered that the perfect career for you is out there, and you don't
know how to transition.

Most women, however, don't know what they want. They
know they don't want to be still doing what they're doing in the
present ten years from now, but they can't quite see what that
future version of themselves is doing instead. Some people have
lost touch with their desires altogether. This is another place
where social conditioning often works against us. There's a bit
of a taboo against being a very ambitious woman—and honestly,
against female desire in general. It's not lady-like to *want*. If you
never know what you want to eat for dinner or which movie
you'd like to see, getting in touch with your desire is going to
be the first step of your reinvention.

DISCOVERY AND EXPLORATION

We often get the message that a good mother, loving wife, or responsible adult puts their desires second after the needs of their children, husband, and duties. Sure, most relationships require a certain amount of sacrifice, but it tends to fall more heavily on women. Ignore your personal desires for long enough, and they go underground.

Now's the time to dig them up.

In this chapter, I'll take you through a series of desire-finding questions and exercises to help you figure out what you want enough to kick a new reinvention cycle into gear. We'll then explore that desire through a series of first low-stakes and then higher-stakes explorations to make sure it's worthy of committing to for the next few years of your professional life.

PHASE 1

For most people, Phase 1 is a series of mini-cycles that go from imagination to education to experimentation and back. The first step in the cycle is easy and should get under your fear radar with no problem because it all happens in your head.

The biggest obstacle you'll likely face in the first step of Phase 1 is your adult rationality. Resist the temptation to start by ruling things out. It's natural to begin where you are and only look at your immediate neighborhood. This is a legitimate exercise, and we'll use it later, but we want to cast the widest possible net and then narrow it down.

One of the women who made the get-out-of-anesthesiology pact with me had the drive and the mental fortitude to start something new. She was brave enough and confident but had no idea what she wanted to do. I remember her saying, "I don't want to be a nurse or a doctor."

"Okay," I said. "What about something outside of medicine?"

She thought about it for a minute. "I don't want to be a paralegal or a lawyer either."

At this stage, it's too early to even be thinking about job titles, much less simply taking the positions you're most familiar with in your field and thinking about their correlates in other professions.

DESIRE-FINDING QUESTIONS

Start with your past. When you were a kid, what did you want to be when you grew up? What did you love doing? If you wanted to impress the twelve-year-old you, what would you tell her you did for a living?

If you won the lottery and had so much money that you never had to work again, after all the celebration and relaxation, when the fun stopped being fun, what would you do with your time?

If I had a magic wand and could pop you over into a parallel universe in which you were living your ideal life, what would you be doing for work?

What do you do, or would you do for free? Do you have hobbies you pursue on the weekend? Do you do any volunteer work?

What inspires you? Be on the lookout for inspiration. The last time I was in Phase 1, I happened to watch a documentary on Ruth Bader Ginsburg, and because my mind was primed to notice interesting people and careers, I briefly considered becoming a lawyer in my next cycle. What she did and what she had to go through to do it was so inspiring that I spun out a little daydream, exploring the idea until I decided it wasn't what I wanted to do next. This wasn't because it seemed impossible but because it didn't tick all the boxes of what I wanted next in my reinvention. RBG fought injustice patiently, quietly, and relentlessly for years, moving the enormous rock of legalized sexism a fraction of an inch at a time. I have tremendous respect for what she did, but I think it would all just make me angry.

What are you curious about? Have you ever gotten lost on Wikipedia or chased information across websites? What kind of clickbait do you fall prey to? What kind of books, magazines, and online articles do you read?

What are your current discontents? What are you feeling an absence of? This has always been a big part of how I've decided what reinvention to take on next. I chose to work at a homeless shelter for my first reinvention cycle because I'd grown dissatisfied with just doing my own thing for myself. I wanted something more fulfilling. And it was fulfilling, but with that itch scratched, I saw that I also wanted something that would give me more financial security. If there's something you know is missing from your life, finding a way to get that need met is a great way to start your reinvention.

DESIRE-FINDING EXERCISES
Brainstorm

This can be fun to do with a friend. A cocktail may help. Your friend's job is to ask you "what if" questions, and your job is not to shoot them down. Try implementing the improv comedy rule of meeting any suggestion or question with "Yes, and..." This means you first agree with any premise your friend proposes and then add something to it that makes it even more interesting, fun, or exciting.

The only acceptable form of rejection here is "That sounds boring." All other objections are excuses. Your goal in this exercise is *not* to be rational or practical. We're not interested in whether the ideas are doable at this point. That will come later.

Right now, implementation is not only irrelevant; it's an obstacle. If I had tried to assess the real possibility of launching a career in TV from my position as an anesthetist, I never would have had one. It would have seemed impossible, but it didn't even take a long time. All we want to know at this point is what sounds fun, interesting, or exciting.

Get a Little List

Jot down a list of everything you enjoy doing, without regard to whether it's a marketable skill. Do you like knitting? It goes on the list. Like drinking wine? Add that too. I'm not promising or even implying you can find a job doing any of these things, but if nothing else, focusing on things that you enjoy will give you a little energy boost. And that's not all!

Mix and Match

Review your list and try combining things in unusual ways. *Dilbert* cartoonist Scott Adams credits his success at his dream job to having put together what he calls a "talent stack." He explains it this way: "I can draw better than most people, but I'm hardly an artist. And I'm not any funnier than the average standup comedian who never makes it big, but I'm funnier than most people. The magic is that few people can draw well *and* write jokes. It's the combination of the two that makes what I do so rare. And when you add in my business background, suddenly I had a topic that few cartoonists could hope to understand without living it."[23]

---

23   Scott Adams, *How to Fail at Almost Everything and Still Win Big: Kind of the Story of My Life* (New York: Portfolio, 2013).

Expose Yourself

If you're coming up empty or not feeling pulled in any particular direction, you can pick an almost random one to start exploring. Scan your LinkedIn connections or think about the people you know socially. Who among them strikes you as interesting? Reach out and ask them about their work. Even if you think you know what they do, get curious. Pretend you're a reporter and interview them about what an average day is like, what they do, and with whom they interact. If one of their colleagues does something that sounds exciting, ask for an introduction. All we're looking for here is a glimmer of interest, a loose thread you can pull.

If absolutely no one you know is interesting or if exploring within your network doesn't yield any good leads, google "Conventions in [your city or the closest medium-to-large city to you]." You can also try "Trade shows" and "Professional Conferences" with the city name. Read through the search results for anything that sounds like it might be interesting. Conventions and conferences are wonderful ways to explore an industry. They tend to cover many different aspects of a field, and they can give you a surprisingly accurate sense of the personalities that work in it. If nothing else, it's excellent confidence training to get out there and learn a few new things around more than a few new people.

Check Your Own Backyard

There's nothing saying reinvention needs to be as dramatic as mine from anesthesiology to TV. If there's a new job title or field you've gotten excited about, get creative, finding ways you might add an element of it to your current work. Create a new position at your current company, or find a company in your industry that already has an element of your new interest area.

Another option is to try googling "disruption" and your current field. I'm guessing that no matter what field you're in, AI and climate change will show up as things that might disrupt your industry. There are probably other more targeted disruptions on the horizon as well. If any of them interest you, you might discover you could learn enough about them, which, paired with your industry-specific knowledge, would turn into a lucrative and exciting consulting job helping companies prepare for or adjust to that disruption.

Window Shopping

Look at any of the platforms that offer online classes. Harvard offers over 150 free online courses on everything from Fundamentals of Neuroscience to Food Fermentation to Omens, Oracles, and Prophecies. The Great Courses online catalog includes American Sign Language, Synthetic Biology, and Video Storytelling. If you can't find a spark of interest in something on those sites, I'd like to gently suggest that you might not just be alienated from your desires but clinically depressed. Please, find some support from a qualified person. Even if you can't act on a new enthusiasm yet, this part of the reinvention cycle should be fun.

Window Selling

If you're looking for something to inject some enthusiasm and energy into your life, consider taking a job in sales. It's not something you'll necessarily feel much desire for, but if nothing else has lit you up, sales is easy to get into, potentially highly profitable, and a skill you'll be able to transfer to anything you later find more desire for.

Have you instantly discounted this suggestion? Are you thinking, *Oh, I could never do sales. I'm way too introverted*, or *I would hate every minute of that. I can't stand being pushy*? Great! The most successful salesperson I know is a quiet, gentle, retiring Vietnamese guy. He sells huge, multimillion-dollar bridge contracts exactly because he's so nice. People trust him.

DESIRE FOUND!

You may not know what you want to do next, but you do want something. You wouldn't have read this far if you didn't. That's fantastic! Tap into that desire, even if it's just a desire for a desire. The process of figuring out what excites you is exciting.

Now, take a moment to feel good about this. Then resolve to make a project out of finding your next project, knowing you're already on your way to reinventing your life. You're already doing the work. Your life is already more interesting.

EXPLORATION

The easiest way to explore something is all in your head. Once your desire-finding turns up something interesting, let your imagination run wild. Daydream about ways it might become what you do as your next reinvention.

Notice I said day*dream*, not day*mare* (as in a daytime nightmare). The goal here isn't to imagine reasons you wouldn't be able to follow a newly discovered interest or to contemplate how exploring it might go terribly wrong and never amount to anything. But this *is* exploration, not fantasy. You can start to let a little sliver of realism in at this stage.

For example, after I left SnapNurse, I started looking for what would be exciting in my next reinvention cycle. I asked myself the first of the desire-finding questions and went look-ing for childhood dreams I might resurrect. I'm going to take you through my entire thought process so you can see how open-ended it is and how it might have flowed from mental exploration into the real-world exploration stage of research.

ROCK STAR!

Like most American kids growing up in the eighties, I wanted to be a rock star. (As a mini-test, did you have this dream too? If you did, did you remember it when you asked yourself the desire-finding questions? Did you dismiss it out of hand as too impractical? If you did, repeat the desire-finding questions and exercises, giving yourself more freedom. You can want absolutely anything. I'm not going to require you to set off on an impossible quest, but I want you to challenge yourself to get the juiciest, most desirable of your desires onto your list. It's a list of *desires*, after all—not a list of options or even possibilities.) Rock star was on my list, so I explored it.

I don't have a rockstar voice. I have a choir-girl voice. It's unfair, but it's true. I could take singing lessons and work on it, but I'm never going to have a belt-it-out rock 'n' roll voice. Additionally, if I could launch a singing career in my mid-fifties and become a rockstar by sixty, would I really want that? I don't think so.

So, is it time for me to move on to the next desire and give up on this one?

Nope. We're exploring.

I dug a little deeper. I asked myself what other careers in the rockstar world might be fun. There are probably a hun-dred different job titles with just one degree of separation from "rock star." Just off the top of my head, I thought of the people who contribute to making music—producers, engineers, session musicians, backup singers, agents, and promoters. Then there are all the fields adjacent to it, like event management, marketing, distribution, and sales. I could have taken my exploration out of my imagination and into the real world at this point and done a simple Google search for something like "careers in music" or "careers in rock music." But my interest had petered out at that point.

Still, if you've worked in accounting, event planning, sales, project management, website design, marketing, or advertising, there are people in your field working adjacent to your wildest dream career—rockstar, astronaut, circus performer, novelist, ballerina—and there's no reason why you couldn't be one of them.

But it still wasn't time for me to give up on the rockstar dream. I asked myself another question: "Why did I want to be a rockstar?" What was it about that career that appealed to me?

I thought about the music videos I used to watch on MTV. My mind took a little side quest into combining my TV background with my rockstar interest. I could make music videos or documentaries or explore what MTV was up to these days. But that wasn't intensely interesting to me either, so I went back to the exploration of why I wanted to be a rockstar.

I remembered videos of singers strutting around the stage and the camera shots that panned out over an audience of thousands. I remembered the documentaries that showed a singer walking through snaking hallways and down a narrow chute that spit them out on stage. Suddenly there they were, in the blazing lights and a wall of sound. *That* was what I wanted. I wanted the adrenaline of performance and the massive rush of an audience pouring energy back at me.

Wow, I thought, *I bet that feels amazing.* Then I thought, *I bet a lot of other people want that feeling too*, and my entrepreneurial training kicked in. I'd identified an unmet need. How could I meet it for myself and others? As I let my mind go down that route, I thought about theme parks where you go to get that kind of lunatic adrenaline thrill, and I thought about karaoke, where people are already living out a rock 'n' roll fantasy. I realized I was imagining the ultimate karaoke experience. I'd pay for that! I bet other people would too.

I kept going, imagining what you'd need. Like karaoke, you could have the people waiting for or recovering from their moment in the spotlight be the audience for the other performers. You'd need a live band with backup singers, dancers, and maybe some costume pieces for people to borrow.

Then I imagined an even more deluxe offering with a stylist, makeup artist, and choreographer on staff so the would-be rockstar could get all kitted out and maybe even rehearse a few times. If something like that existed, I have a friend who I know would plunk down some serious money to give her lawyer husband that kind of rockstar experience for his birthday.

I hope you see how this kind of exploration almost immediately makes your life more fun and interesting, and it's totally free. If the next time I met a friend for coffee, we found we didn't have that much catching up to do, I could say, "Hey, here's an idea I've been playing with," and we'd have a great time thinking about the different kinds of bespoke wishes we could stage.

This is exactly the path I took at the start of my TV reinvention. I'd always wanted to be in Hollywood. I'd watched the Academy Awards and Golden Globes or the Emmys and wondered if I could ever be a part of that world. So I decided to find out.

FIRST DATES

Like first dates in real life, you may feel a little nervous at this point, but (at least in theory) your excitement about what might be possible will get you over any trepidation. You can also dial your initial investment up or down by dipping your toes in with online research or going full throttle with an internship or part-time job in your new field of interest.

On a career first date, you're investing a little more time in something you've found interesting. You're exploring options and doing research, looking for the answers to two key questions: "Would I like this as much as I think I would?" and "How might I make it happen?"

Sometimes you'll find out quickly that this one's a dud or that logistics make it not worth seeing that one again. Sometimes, you'll go on another date or three. If, at any point, you realize this isn't the reinvention for you, you can go back to the first step with a little more information about what you do and don't want. On the other hand, if you can't stop thinking about a date you didn't see a second time because you lived thousands of miles apart, put it back on the list. In Chapter 8, we'll look at alternate routes and shortcuts. The emphasis in Phase 1 must stay on *Is it interesting?* Then, when you've found a reinvention you think you could get serious about, you're into Phase 2.

LOW-STAKES DATES

When I was in the first phase of my second reinvention cycle, I moved from Huntington to Newport Beach and worked at a homeless shelter for battered women and children, which was rewarding but depressing. Later, I moved into teaching, which was rewarding and not depressing but didn't pay me enough to quit waiting tables. I knew what I was looking for in my next reinvention: money. That big, exciting desire pushed me out of Phase 0 when I was starting to feel lost again.

I knew I didn't want to be a nurse, but I thought I could leverage my premed undergraduate degree into a better-paying career in something less than the dozen years it would take me to become a doctor. So, I hitched up the horse and buggy and went down to the library.

Okay, maybe it wasn't so long ago that there weren't cars, but it was before the internet made research an at-home activity. Today, you can probably get at least a date or two's worth of information from the comfort of your phone. Nonetheless, your public library is still a great resource, and librarians are almost universally helpful people.

Research

Whether the possibility that has you excited is more like my ultimate karaoke idea or the one that took me to the library to research jobs in the medical profession, try to think about the domain your interest is pointing you toward. For the former, I could research bespoke entertainment and read up on party planners and event management. For the latter, I researched job titles. The distinction here is whether you want to do something that already exists or need to create something new. In the second step of Phase 1, the reinvention cycle is a little different if it involves inventing the company where you'll work, and I'll cover that in the next section, the Trip Test, but for everyone, the question you're looking to answer in the early dating stage of research is "How might I...?"

When I went to the library, my question was "How might I quickly leverage my undergraduate premed degree into a job that pays well?"

I researched careers in medicine and the required degrees, looking for something that seemed interesting and would triple my salary. I rejected "physician assistant" and "lab tech." Then I came across "anesthesiologist assistant" and thought, *Oh, that sounds interesting.* To be honest, I had no idea what anesthesiology was, so I dug a little deeper. I looked at pictures and watched a few videos, and decided that yes, in fact, it was interesting. And it had a starting salary of $65,000. This was very interesting indeed, considering I was making $20,000 as a teacher at the time.

I did some more research and learned there were two paths to becoming an anesthesiologist assistant: I could go to nursing school and get a bachelor's degree, followed by two years in the ICU and another two in anesthesia school, or I could get a master's degree in anesthesiology. By the first route, I'd end up as a nurse with a specialization in anesthesiology. By the second, I'd become an anesthetist, which was more like being a PA (physician's assistant). Both jobs paid about the same, but the second path was faster, and I was in a hurry. But there was a hitch—two, actually. Unlike nursing school, I'd have to take the MCAT to get into a master's program, and at the time, only two schools in the country offered such programs. Still, I declared victory. I'd answered the *How might I* question. I'd found a job title and two educational paths to it.

Another way to research the *How might I* question is to prowl LinkedIn looking for people who already have the job you want. If someone—*anyone*—is doing what you want to as a career, then it's a job that's possible to get, and there's probably more than one path to getting it.

If I'd continued to be interested in following in the footsteps of RBG, I would have checked Wikipedia for the current crop of Supreme Court justices and researched what their backgrounds had in common. I would have looked at what was different about how they each got where they are and explored the different paths they took. I might have even dug a little deeper and investigated the backgrounds of top contenders for the next vacant seat.

Of course, not all interesting jobs will show up in a library search. In the next section on slightly higher-stakes future dating, I'll recommend local industry conferences and a few other lines of research, so if you don't find a job title that excites you in your library research, don't give up! Some jobs just aren't going to show up there, and some don't exist until you invent them.

Brainstorming Revisited

I have a friend whose daughter was passionately interested in the global environmental crisis. As so many of us do when we're young, she fell in love at first sight and made a serious commitment without dating around much. She spent four years of her life (and quite a lot of her mom's money) getting an environmental science degree only to hit the job market and realize the only even reasonably paid jobs in her field were at oil companies—working for the enemy.

She did some soul-searching and desire-finding and eventually went back to school to study animation. Fair enough, but I would have encouraged her to spend a little time brainstorming before she dismissed the entire industry. She could have spent a date or two's worth of time asking *How might I use my experience and degree to make a good living doing something to help the environment?*

She could have coupled her degree with her interest in film and gone to work for *National Geographic*, documenting the changing climate. She might have started a consulting company to advise businesses on ways to reduce their carbon footprint.

If you love a field but can only find jobs in it that you're not excited by, get creative. Brainstorm ways of combining your interest in that field with other interests you have. Try coming at things from the opposite direction. Think of the job titles already on your résumé and brainstorm what a similar function might look like in this new industry.

Finally, if you're still working on your confidence creation and want not just low-stakes exploration but a low-stakes reinvention, take another hard look at your current situation. No matter how bored you are with your job, someone out there would love to replace you. Look at what you do from their point of view. What would make it appealing to them? What made it attractive to you when you first applied for it? Brainstorm everything you can come up with to make your current job as exciting or meaningful as you can. That might mean going back into an office when you've been working remotely, trying for a promotion, or becoming a mentor to those enthusiastic new hires.

THE TRIP TEST

I have a friend who swears she'll never again get serious about a guy until she's gone on two out-of-town trips with him. Something about getting a person away from their normal routine and familiar environment shows you who they are. She says the trick is to take two trips. You plan one, and he plans the other. If you're all about hiking and skiing and he's a tropical-drinks-brought-to-you-poolside guy, it's good to know that up front. From cross-country road trips to international flights, travel is also a great way to ensure that something goes wrong, revealing how the relationship does under strain.

These dates take a larger investment of time and money, so you wouldn't want to go on them with just anyone. The same is true for the second (and last) level of exploration in Phase 1 before we make a commitment and move into Phase 2.

Courses

Whether you've gotten excited about an industry, a job title, a subject, or a skillset, there's probably a twelve-week course on it that you can take at night or on weekends for under a thousand dollars. You can do this through your local community college or university (often without having to enroll formally) or online through a platform like Coursera, Lynda, or the Great Courses, or through an established university like Harvard or Stanford.

You can certainly find shorter courses and free ones, but the whole point of these more time- and money-intensive Phase 1 Step 2 "road trip" dates is to test whether your new interest will stand up to more investment. If you're curious about several areas of study, the shorter, free classes are a great low-stakes research option, but to vet a new interest for Phase 2, I'd encourage you to make a bigger (but still very modest) investment.

This "take a course" test doesn't have to be academic. If you always wanted to be a chef, take a cooking class. If you rediscovered a childhood passion for horses, take a riding class. You don't have to know yet how these might turn into your next career. We'll do some reality testing in Phase 2. Remember, Phase 1 is all about desire—finding, exploring, and testing it.

If you get five weeks into a thirteen-week course and discover the desire's dead, that's great! You've probably picked up a few interesting tidbits, enjoyed yourself, and learned something about what you do and don't want. This is not failure! It's not even a dead end. Go back to the desire-finding questions, particularly the last one, "What are your discontents?" and add to the list whatever it was about your most recent reinvention possibility that you found lacking or annoying. Don't buy into that masculine, linear "happily ever after" narrative. This is a happy ending. You got out early from something that didn't hold your interest. That's a huge win!

I did this with both my first and fourth reinvention cycles. I explored social work and teaching for two years before reinventing myself as an anesthetist. When I reinvented myself as an entrepreneur, I explored a fractional hotel booking app before I committed to SnapNurse. Each exploration helped refine and create the final successful reinvention.

Conferences

I've already recommended attending local conventions and conferences to expose yourself to new industries. As a late-stage Phase 1 activity, it can make sense to travel to attend one that targets your new interest rather than browsing only the local options.

Because conferences are designed to be both educational and networking events, they're ideal venues for late Phase 1 exploration. Go. Learn everything and meet everyone you can. Even if you end up deciding this isn't the industry for you, you'll leave with a set of new contacts and a download of information that can end up cross-pollinating in productive and fascinating ways down the line.

As a total and unabashed newbie, you're also in a terrific position to get the most out of a conference. Once people have been in an industry for a while, a certain amount of hierarchy and status management becomes part of every experience. But you're exempt and can gleefully sit at the bottom of the pecking order and learn from everyone. Saying "I don't know anything about the industry, but I've done some research, and I think it's really cool; I want to learn as much as possible about what it might be like to work in your field," is a great way to open a conversation with anyone wearing a conference badge.

These conferences are usually held over a long weekend, so you might have to take a day or two off work, but don't let the logistics or expense stop you. This is an excellent confidence-training exercise, a fantastic way to vet an interest, and can easily turn into a shortcut through much of Phase 2. That's what's happened to me.

I didn't know anything about TV. I just thought it sounded exciting. The Peachtree Film Festival was coming up in Atlanta, where I lived, so I registered and went. It was almost a low-stakes date because I didn't have to travel, but it ended up being such a fast track to working in television that it ended my first phase and took me halfway through the second.

Not knowing how I might fit into the industry, I sat in on a screenwriting class led by Mark Brown, the writer of two successful TV shows, *Barbershop* and *Two Can Play That Game*. After the class, I went up to talk to him. "What you do sounds so interesting!" I said. "How did you get into it?"

We talked for a few minutes before he said, "Look, I want to continue this conversation, but I have this meeting with A&E Networks right now."

I was all ready to ask if I could meet him after and trade him a drink for an info dump when he added, "You can come along if you want."

I went.

I got at least a year's worth of education sitting there watching Mark pitch A&E, and I immediately understood why it's called "pitching." Mark didn't have anything written down. He just lobbed idea after idea at the exec like spitballs at a wall, hoping one would stick. It was thrilling, and watching him, I thought, *This is it! This is what I want to do.*

Interns, Shadows, and Others

There's no better way to learn than by doing. For five years, my daughter knew she wanted to be a chef. She got an internship as a chef's assistant. She no longer wants to be a chef. Again, this is a great outcome! If she hadn't tried it out, she might have spent four years (at $53,000 a year) at the Culinary Institute of America only to graduate and make the same discovery.

This is not to say that all internships are negative experiences. I know many young people who got an internship during the summer between their junior and senior years in college and were hired by the same company when they graduated. My point is that regardless of the outcome, internships are a great litmus test. If you like the work, you'll walk away with professional contacts in your field of interest, if not a standing job offer. If you hate the work, you'll get out early and probably with some great stories.

The biggest downside of internships is that they're hard to get if you're not a student. But there are a few easy workarounds. You can find someone to shadow for a week. This is a well-established practice in medicine. We regularly had students shadowing us when I worked in anesthesiology, and I have a friend who told me her son's pediatrician was rarely without a shadow. This can be trickier to negotiate in big companies where HR may throw up obstacles, but many small businesses or self-employed professionals will be happy to let you hang out in the background and watch them do what they do for a few days.

You can also look for part-time or temporary work in your

industry of interest. You might not be able to do the job you're considering this way, but offering to be someone's part-time assistant or subbing in for a vacationing employee can get you close to highly placed people. If a part-time role is not already established, offer to work for free. Getting close enough to the action to see if you'd enjoy doing it yourself is well worth your time. I'll go into how to get this kind of work in more detail when I talk about finding a mentor, but the kernel is this: always have something to offer. Approach asking for part-time, temporary, or volunteer work in your dream industry not from the place of why you need the experience but from why they need your help. Yes, you want to do your research, but they want someone who'll answer the phones or take some of their work off their plate. Be that someone.

Entrepreneurs

Several different desire streams feed into the pool of aspiring entrepreneurs. If your desire-finding dreams were all about jobs or industries that don't yet exist, or if your current discontents all boil down to "I don't want to work for anyone else," entrepreneurship may be what kicks off your next reinvention cycle.

There seems to be a particular kind of person who's well-suited to this sort of adventure. In fact, if you have an entrepreneurial personality, it may be the only path you'll enjoy, and you'll likely take it cycle after cycle as a serial entrepreneur.

If you're like most of us, the *what* doesn't matter as much as the *how*, which is why late-stage exploration often continues the one before it, brainstorming and researching at a deeper level.

When I was getting my fourth reinvention cycle going, I knew I wanted to start my own business, and I knew I wanted to do something in tech. I was excited about being a tech entrepreneur, so I headed into this stage with the question "What are the different industries I could try to disrupt that tech hasn't already revolutionized?"

If that's where you are, I advise starting by leveraging your past. It's a lesson I learned the hard way. Near the end of my TV career, I got an invitation to pitch Playboy TV. The idea was just so outrageous that I had to take the meeting.

I started brainstorming shows in that narrow sliver of overlap between what I'd be willing to work on and what Playboy might want to buy. I found out about love hotels—fractional booking establishments that rent rooms by the hour for, well, you can probably guess. My idea was to pitch this as a travel show. We'd go around the world and tour these hotels. Some are wild, with themed rooms and rates rivaling the Ritz. With over thirty thousand of them in Japan alone, we wouldn't run out of material anytime soon.

Playboy passed on the idea, but later, when I was kicking around ideas for a startup with my brother and looking for an industry to disrupt, I remembered the research I'd done. Now, if I'd come up with the idea to disrupt the hotel industry by convincing ordinary people to rent out rooms in their houses to strangers, I might have gotten ahead of Vrbo and Airbnb. Instead, I thought, *Love hotels are a $40 billion industry in Japan and don't exist anywhere else.*

My idea wasn't to start a chain of love hotels in the US. I didn't want to do anything that seedy, but I did a little more research and realized how often hotel rooms were empty during the day. I put that together with how many people work from Starbucks and thought, *A fractional booking app for hotels!* People could rent a hotel room for a few hours at a time and have a quiet place with a desk, a phone, and a coffee maker to work. Provided they checked out before 4:00, the same room could be rented again that night. Snuzo made it out of Phase 1 and into Phase 2. It probably shouldn't have.

So I went back to Phase 1, brainstorming and researching, and this time I followed the advice I've given you. My friend Mark Brown suggested I pivot the app into a field that I knew well and that was nursing and the challenges around staffing. I knew the profession, the personality profiles of people who went into it, and their different specializations. I understood the different types of credentialing nurses need and how the hiring process works at hospitals.

Remember, back in Chapter 2, when I said nothing is wasted? If you didn't believe me, then here's more evidence. How did I disrupt nurse staffing? I took the idea of fractional hotel room rentals from my hugely unsuccessful first booking-app entrepreneurial venture and applied it to nurses. I knew Snuzo's code and booking structure was poorly built, but I learned from it and hired a different engineering team and CTO to create an entirely new structure. I took what I learned from the failure of Snuzo and applied it to SnapNurse.

Start Where You Are

What frustrates you about the industry you're in? Many great businesses start with someone thinking *I really wish someone would...* And then doing whatever that is themselves.

This is how my brother reinvented his career. He was working as a baby-maker—err, I mean embryologist. He spent all day in a lab putting eggs and sperm together to create embryos for people who were having trouble conceiving. He was starting to get bored with the work and frustrated with how difficult it was first to get the specimens and then the embryos shipped quickly enough. *I wish someone would build tech-enabled short-term storage,* he thought. Then he did exactly that.

He's still an embryologist, but instead of working for a doctor, he now works for himself and has doctors and clinics as clients.

If you're in a career where you've found yourself thinking *Wouldn't it be great if someone offered X service or invented a gadget that did Y?* you probably have a great start for an entrepreneurial venture. Nobody outside Sean's field was sitting around ruminating on whether there was an easier way to keep embryos cold. It was only because he was in the industry that he knew his idea would be a big deal, something that everyone in his small, niche field needed and would be delighted to have— and pay him to provide.

Not only does solving a problem you've had in your field make your startup more likely to solve a problem other people have (which Snuzo did not), but you'll also be able to speak to your clients and customers in their language.

Start Further Afield

This doesn't mean that you can't do very well solving a problem outside the industry where you currently work. The four Stanford students who founded DoorDash weren't guys who'd worked in the restaurant industry for years, thinking *I wish someone would come up with a way to deliver our food to our customers.* The problem they were trying to solve was one familiar to most college students—*I wish someone would bring me food!*

If you've found an idea in a field you don't have much professional experience in, you're going to need to do quite a lot of research while you're still in Phase 1. Stay open to ditching the idea you're exploring and starting over with brainstorming either a different problem to solve or a different way of solving the same problem.

As an example, if I were going to take my ultimate karaoke idea on this kind of Phase 1 exploratory road trip, I'd start by brainstorming different ways I might solve the "I want to experience what it's like to be a rock star" problem. I could try a pop-up model, almost like a concert tour that travels around the country doing a few nights in different cities. I could make it a stand-alone place, possibly in a destination city like Las Vegas or LA. I could base it on the private-event model as a package-deal fundraiser or birthday party. I'd then research these different models. How do traveling Broadway shows or circuses work? How does Disney or Six Flags make its money? Who do people like Jeff Bezos or Beyoncé hire to throw their galas or birthday parties?

On the other hand, if I knew what industry I wanted to disrupt but didn't have much personal experience, I'd start attending conferences. I'd go to every panel or workshop on the industry's future, particularly future disruptions they were anticipating, and I'd ask everyone I could buttonhole, *What's your biggest frustration? What gets in the way of you doing your job?*

WARNING SIGNS

If you're doing it right, getting stuck in Phase 1 is hard. Desire-finding and exploration are inherently exciting, and that excitement will usually propel you into Phase 2. In fact, the biggest risk in Phase 1 isn't that you'll stay here too long but that you'll skip over the research and experimentation and commit yourself too deeply too soon.

That said, some people do get addicted to dreaming. The same things that make Phase 1 manageable can make it too comfortable. All the things that we talked about in Chapter 3 can still stop you here. It takes courage to cross into the next phase. Especially if you have some trauma or have lost confidence through repeated disappointments or social conditioning, Phase 1 can be a very appealing place to stay.

If you've been frustrated about your life for a long time, you may be happier here than you've been in years. Moving on to Phase 2 and committing to your reinvention may be scary, but you can do it. Phase 2 starts with a reality and resources check that protects you from many of the things that probably scare you, and every step we take is a baby step. I'm never going to ask you to jump into anything headfirst. We'll dip our toes into the new, and keep up our tiptoe around fear.

The other danger that can crop up in Phase 1 is forgetting that nothing is wasted and failure is impossible. You're dating your future. Going on one date and not a second is a success. Everything you experiment with and explore helps refine your vision of your desired future. When you're shoe shopping, you don't fail every time you try on a pair you don't buy. You're being selective about your next career because you deserve to have one you love.

CHAPTER SUMMARY

In Phase 1, you discover desire, explore interests, and test them through a series of mini-cycles of imagination, education, and experimentation. It's important to let your imagination run free at first. Use desire-finding questions and exercises to uncover childhood dreams, innate interests, curiosities, and discontents, then explore what you've discovered through low-stakes online research and higher-investment "first dates" like courses, conferences, and internships.

Ask "How might I...?" and look for paths to your new goal. Research job titles, brainstorm combinations of interests, and consider starting a business of your own by looking at what frustrates you in your current industry or focusing on a problem you could solve. Finally, test your interest by making investments of time and money.

As you get more in touch with what you really want and start finding ways that you might create a much more interesting and exciting future, you'll have more energy and positivity. With a future you're ready to get serious about, it's time to move into Phase 2. But first, congratulations! You're already more interesting. You have new things to talk about when you meet friends for coffee. You have more energy and enthusiasm about your future. You're probably already less irritable and bored and having more fun. Let's keep it moving forward!

Chapter 7

PHASE 2, PREPARATION

MY SHORTEST RAMP-UP THROUGH PHASE 2 INVOLVED taking on debt and going to school full-time for two years in a program so intense that we were prohibited from having an outside job. In my subsequent reinvention, I spent a lot longer in this phase. I was lucky to have a career that needed people around the clock, so I was able to arrange my first job's schedule around my second. I did anesthesia full-time during the week and spent my weekends trawling the back roads of the South for characters, filming them, and editing tapes. Later, I reversed the split, putting in twelve-hour anesthesiology shifts Friday through Sunday and working in TV Monday through Friday. It was exhausting! I remember sitting on the edge of my bed to take off my tennis shoes and waking up the next morning with all the lights lit and my shoes still on my feet.

If I hadn't gone into first anesthesiology and then TV with so much enthusiasm, I might have given up before I made it through Phase 2. But I was totally in love with the idea of my reinvention and knew I couldn't graduate from Emory or break into TV by doing anything less.

PREPARATION AND COMMITMENT

Phase 2 always starts with desire—the excitement of a new passion bubbling over from imagination into action. If in Phase 1 you were dating possible futures, in Phase 2, you put a ring on it. It's the "Ready, Set" that will be followed by Phase 3's "Go!"

It's important to come into this phase with energy and enthusiasm because you'll need it to sustain you through the ups and downs of building your new life while you're still living your old one. In fact, a big part of the work of Phase 2 is done to shepherd and preserve the energy and excitement you come into it with.

In this chapter, we'll start doing that work, preparing for your reinvention by checking your assumptions, resources, and obligations so you don't commit to something truly impossible. (But wildly ambitious is fine!) With an initial inventory done, the next step is to understand what you don't know yet that you'll need to learn before you start living your dream. Then you'll make a commitment to your new future and get ready to leap into your new life.

REALITY CHECK

Before you make the kind of commitment that Phase 2 requires, it's important to audit what bringing your dream to fruition is likely to cost and evaluate whether you can pay it. It can be very tempting to skip over this step. It may feel like signing a prenup or going in for premarital counseling. You're excited! You want to sweep into your new life on the wings of your passion for it.

I get it. But I promise you it's worth inventorying your resources and estimating the investments. Your enthusiasm will falter, and if all you have to shore up your determination is how you felt eighteen months ago, you might lose your confidence. In those inevitable moments, knowing you did a sober calculus of what it would take and made a rational determination that it was possible might just save your dream.

INVENTORIES

People talk about having a work–life balance like it's possible to untangle the two. Maybe if you were living in a fantasy of a 1950s businessman's life with a housewife for your house and a full-time mother for your kids, it would be possible to compartmentalize your life that tidily. For those of us living in the real world, it's not.

You have responsibilities you can't just ignore. Maybe you have kids or a partner who needs your time and attention. Maybe your confidence is still at a low ebb, or your finances are depleted. None of that makes reinvention impossible, but not accounting for it makes it more likely to fail.

WHAT PERSONAL OBLIGATIONS AND RESOURCES DO YOU HAVE?

The question here isn't *What do the people in your life expect of you?* but *What is your true, personal sense of what you owe the people in your life?* It's important to meet your own standards, but it's equally (if not more) important *not* to meet standards imposed on you by social conventions or family habits, particularly if you're already harboring some resentment around them.

If your kids are used to having you pick them up from school every day, but they spend the whole drive playing games on their iPads, pay a neighborhood kid with a driver's license to do the school run and free up hours to make a dent in your reinvention.

On the other hand, if eating dinner with your family, a monthly date night with your partner, brunch with your friends, attending your kid's weekend soccer games, or hosting Thanksgiving for your extended family is truly important to you, you should exclude an hour every weekday, four hours every fourth Friday or second Sunday, two hours each Saturday in the Spring and Fall, or the whole month of November from your inventory of hours available to work toward your new dream.

In either case, I strongly recommend talking to the people in your life about the personal reinvention you're beginning. Let your family know they still matter, and you still love them, but that you're doing something exciting that will make you much happier. Help them see how they'll benefit from it too.

When you talk to your family, tell them about the weeknight dinners or monthly date nights you've already set aside. Maybe there's something more important to them. You can easily make a trade if they'd rather take a two-week vacation with you than lose you to the kitchen, pies, and turkey.

Tell your friends too. If you don't, you'll start hearing "Where are you? What are you doing? How come you're not spending time with us anymore?" If they're real friends who want what's best for you, they'll not only understand when you explain your plan to start spending all your free time writing music but encourage you and show up to your first open mic. They'll enjoy hearing about what you're learning and be curious about your adventures. They might want to help with the work, contribute their expertise, or even invest financially in your startup.

Having a friend or family member who believes in you and will even do a bit of cheerleading when you start to waver is an invaluable resource, so enlist this kind of support in advance. Ruth Bader Ginsburg always credits her husband's unflagging support for part of her willingness to face down the sexism that tried to stop her at every step of her climb to the Supreme Court. If you have that kind of partner, lean on them. If you don't, ask your most optimistic friend or an upbeat coworker to remind you about how much you want to make this change happen and pump you up when your motivation goes flat.

On the other hand, if you have people in your network who you know might be inclined to add their weight of judgment when you're feeling overwhelmed, ask them in advance for their patience. Tell them, "I want to hear your thoughts, and I value your opinion, but I'm on this path, and it's going to take some time, so please give me a couple of years before you start raising any doubts you have."

Even so, there may be times as you move through the intense work of Phase 2 when you feel like your friends aren't supporting you as much as you expected them to. If this happens, don't retreat deeper into your cave and lick your wounds; ask your friends about it. You may find that they're all talking about how amazing they think you are and how much they admire what you're doing, but the message isn't getting back to you.

WHAT FINANCIAL OBLIGATIONS AND RESOURCES DO YOU HAVE?

Take a good look at your expenses. You'll probably save some money not going out during this phase, but you may spend more to have meals delivered. You may also need to invest in your education. In the next step, you'll estimate what Phase 2 will likely cost, but don't be afraid to invest in yourself and your future at this stage. If you want to get into management but determine you'll need an MBA, don't rule that reinvention out because the degree costs $40,000 a year.

On the other hand, make sure whatever degree you think you need is truly necessary. I'd bet many prominent people with the job you want advanced through the ranks without a degree. There are nontraditional routes to the top, and for positions requiring an advanced degree, it isn't unusual to get your tuition paid by the company for which you're working. You might be able to move into a lower-tier job in the industry you aspire to and support yourself while you climb the ladder to the point that the company is happy to invest in your education.

If you have a mortgage, you want to make sure you can continue to pay it, but you can probably take out a home equity loan to help pay for your education, whether it's university tuition or the cost of starting a business. If you have retirement savings, you can dip into that. Don't let money keep you from creating the reinvention you want, but be practical. Recognize that you'll probably have to live lean for a few years and that you may have to move more slowly through this phase than you'd like to. You might need to do a two-year program in three years and work part-time or start your new business as more of a side hustle than a full-time commitment.

If, on the other hand, you have financial resources, look for ways to leverage them to cut down on the length of time you need to spend in this phase. We'll talk more about this in Phase 3, but I'm a huge believer in deliberately making a distinction between all the nonwork things you do that are meaningful and those that are just distractions. Often, you'll be able to start making more money more quickly if you pay to have someone else do the grocery shopping, clean the house, or manage your logistics. You can also hire expertise rather than learning all the skills you might need to start a business. If you can afford to build a team, you can skip some of the learning curve, but make sure you run the numbers first!

WHAT PROFESSIONAL OBLIGATIONS AND RESOURCES DO YOU HAVE?

This may be controversial, but if you're starting up your next reinvention cycle while still working a forty-hour week, I recommend taking the time now to figure out the minimums required to avoid getting fired. Can you drop from forty hours to thirty? Can you work from home to save yourself the commute time? Meet your professional obligations, but this isn't the time to go above and beyond at work unless your reinvention plan is to create a new job at your present company.

Inventory your professional resources. I'll bet you have many you're not aware of and don't have a few that you're going to need.

When SnapNurse hit Phase 3 (ultrafast growth), it was scaling up so quickly that I couldn't hire people fast enough. I started calling up all the nurses I was friends with to draft them into joining me. I was stunned by how often people told me they weren't qualified. They thought they'd lost any professional resources they once had because they'd been out of the workforce for a few years raising kids. This is nonsense. Raising kids *is* a professional qualification.

Résumé Reframing

If you've been a mom, you have experience managing multiple schedules, organizing complex logistics, and motivating recalcitrant underlings. You've been a teacher, and you've led training. You're almost certainly a skilled multitasker with extraordinary patience and a nurturing presence. These are marketable skills!

If you've thrown birthday parties or planned vacations, you have party-planning and event-management experience. If you've taken care of aging parents, you've done eldercare. If you've managed the family budget, kept all the bills paid, and done your taxes, you have basic bookkeeping skills. You also have years of experience in advertising and entertainment, even if only on the consumer side. If you've had to sell your kids on brushing their teeth or your partner on doing their share of the household tasks, you have sales skills. Many of the best sales-people out there are moms.

Maybe you're not a mom, but you've worked as a waitress or bartender. You can add "works well under pressure," "managed multiple projects on asynchronous timelines," "effective communication," and "customer relations" to your list of professional resources.

Remember, nothing is wasted! Look back over your life with the right squint, and you'll see a host of skills and experiences that you can take with you as you ramp up your next (or first!) career reinvention.

Get a Group

As wonderful as it is to have a personal support network, you need a professional one too. This can be anything from a new friendship with one or two other people with the same or similar jobs in your next-cycle industry to an international professional organization. There are three strong reasons for this: emotional support, learning, and networking.

If you're a TV producer, only another TV producer is going to understand what you're going through. Whether they've been doing it for more or less time than you have, they've had different experiences and probably learned different things from them—from coping techniques to technical ones. They will also have worked with a different set of people and be able to warn you away from some and introduce you to others.

This is important for everyone but most crucial for entrepreneurs. We'll talk more about their unique stresses in a moment, but the sooner you can start building this kind of support for yourself, the better. The most widely known of such groups is YEO (Young Entrepreneurs' Organization), but you must be bringing in a million a year in revenue to join, so it isn't set up to support people just starting out. There are smaller and local groups (and probably some specifically for women) that will be a great source of support, information, and contacts.

Whether starting your own company or targeting an established job title, industry conferences are a great way to learn about existing organizations and make new friendships. If you're lucky, one of these might develop into an informal mentorship with someone more experienced who can encourage you to stay the course or point out a new direction. We'll talk more about mentorship in the second half of Phase 2, but of all the professional relationships you can develop, a mentor will do more for you than any other, and now isn't too early to start looking around for one.

This is one of the few places in life where women have an advantage. Of course, I'm generalizing, but I think women make friends and connections more easily, and even though we can be fiercely ambitious, we're less likely to cut each other down to get ahead. Over and over again in my life, I've leaned on and supported other women. I'm not going to tell you it makes up for systemic sexism, but it's an enormous asset. Make sure you're not leaving such a gift on the table.

INVESTMENTS

The work of Phase 2 is preparation, so the second assessment you need to make isn't of what you have but of what you'll need and what it will cost.

What do you need to know to do what you want to do? This is a question that you'll need to answer for yourself with research, but broadly speaking, there are four ways to acquire the knowledge you'll need to complete your transition from old career to new.

FORMAL EDUCATION

All jobs require specialized knowledge and skills, but some require formal proof that you have it. If the job you want requires an advanced degree, license, or certification, you'll need to get some formal education. Stories of daring frauds aside, if you want to practice law, fly a plane, perform surgery, or open a bar, you'll only get there legally through official channels. Do your research. How much will this training cost? How long will it take? Where is it offered? Are there entrance requirements? There may be some wiggle room on all these points, but before you commit to your new path, it's good to know, on average, what it costs in time and money to get the necessary qualifications so you can budget appropriately.

APPRENTICESHIP

When I showed up at the Peachtree Film Festival, I sat in on a writing class because I thought it might be fun to write TV shows. There are thousands of screenwriting programs in the US in colleges and universities (and independent of them), so I could have gone the formal education route. I could have, but

I didn't have to. The same is true for artists and programmers, chefs, and craftspeople.

If you can learn by doing, you can move into your new profession through a formal or informal apprenticeship. Again, do your research. Look for people on LinkedIn who have the job you want, and find out how they got there. Better yet, see if you can take a few to coffee and ask. The key difference between these jobs and ones that require a formal education is that the skillset matters more than the degree. If an audience, portfolio, resume, or pitch is the way through the gatekeepers, you can pay for classes, work for free, or some combination of the two.

SELF-DIRECTED LEARNING

Informal or self-directed education is another way to pick up the knowledge you need to enter other professions, especially if the reinvention you're planning is a progression from or tangential to your current job. You can combine academic non-degree-seeking programs and not-for-credit courses with hands-on training, part-time work, an internship, and an apprenticeship to construct your own learning program.

The biggest danger of this kind of education is that you won't know when you're done. Do the research ahead of time and be very clear with yourself about what skills you need to acquire to do the job you want. I took this route to becoming a private school teacher because I didn't want to take the formal route of getting a teaching certificate. Instead, I taught myself lesson planning, brushed up on the relevant courses I'd taken in college, and learned how to design fun experiments for my students.

ENTREPRENEURSHIP

Finally, if you want to start your own company, your education comes from starting your own company. There are entrepreneurship programs at most universities, but their primary advantage is offering you a framework for starting your own company. The only criterion for a successful startup is profitability. There are no gatekeepers. There's just the market.

COST-BENEFIT ANALYSIS

Don't let the numbers intimidate you, but as part of your research, figure out what it will cost to learn what you need to know to do what you want to do.

In entrepreneurship, it's having a minimum viable product. In my TV career, I was editing my own pitch tapes. For anesthesiology, it was a master's degree. There's a huge difference between what it cost for me to make a pitch tape and what it cost to make even the leanest possible version of my nursing app. But money spent on education—whatever form your education takes—isn't really spent so much as invested in your future earning ability.

I flew through this phase on my way to my teaching job, and it cost almost nothing. Emory was expensive, but I got scholarships and student loans. I'd started making a little money as an apprentice in TV after three months of working for free, but SnapNurse took two years and cost $100K before I had anything to test in the market.

Of course, there are costs in time as well as money. Having inventoried your resources, figure out how much of each you can devote to powering your reinvention cycle. If time is limited and you have only four hours on each weekend day, and two hours every Wednesday night, that's fine. If it's just forty-five minutes a day while your youngest naps, that's okay too. If you can't afford to spend more than gas money on your reinvention or if every nickel you spend must be raised or borrowed, that's okay too.

Time and money are interdependent, and a surplus of one can compensate for a deficit of the other. You can save a lot of time not learning how to code by hiring a coder. You can save money by not paying for film school but working for minimum wage as a production assistant.

Don't give up on or defer any reinvention you're excited about because you think it will take too long or cost too much. The energy that comes from being very excited about your big dream can easily make up the difference.

INTENTION

Now it's time to commit. Here is where you stop saying "I'm going to" and start saying "I am."

I am attending school.

I am taking an online class.

I am working in TV.

I am pursuing a medical career.

I am starting a company.

If you don't do this, inertia will set in. "Someday, maybe later" will resurface and swallow your dream and all the excitement it's generated. You'll slide back into Phase 0—stuck and stopped by fear.

Yes, this is scary. No, it doesn't have to be as dramatic as quitting teaching and moving from LA to Georgia for graduate school. When I did the research, I realized there was no part-time path to becoming an anesthetist. It was all or nothing, so I went all in. But you can move into Phase 3 in baby steps. That's what I did when I kept a full-time job at the beginning of both my television and my entrepreneurial reinventions.

Going to motivational seminars and getting all pumped up can feel great, but I don't go in for the all-or-nothing fire-walking mentality. Sure, go 100 percent into your next adventure if you want to, and you can, but be practical. If you're a single mom with two kids, you may only give 20 percent of yourself to your reinvention. That doesn't make it any less real and important.

Work also tends to expand to fill the space available to it. After exiting SnapNurse, I went back into Phase 1 and brainstormed my next adventure. I started doing research into the venture capital world. I set up a few meetings as low-stakes "dates," but suddenly, people were throwing companies at me from all sides. I found myself once again working all day, taking meeting after meeting. It was more of a time commitment than I wanted to make.

Venture capital was insisting we elope, so I broke it off. My research taught me that, like medical school, it was something you couldn't experiment with or ease into. It needed a higher commitment level than I was willing to make, and I didn't love it as much as I'd thought I might. I got frustrated by founders who weren't willing to take advice, and I hated turning down people when they asked for an investment. Doing the Phase 1 work of desire-finding and exploring saved me from throwing myself into a reinvention I would not have enjoyed. If I had continued down that road, I would not only have committed money but also obligated myself to those startups until they exited, which could have taken years. I didn't because it didn't pass the energy test.

In the second half of Phase 2, the important things are that you set your intention to keep the cycle moving toward that exciting, energizing new job, that you commit to using the resources you've earmarked for your reinvention on it and nothing else, that you know how you're going to start, and that you commit to not quitting until you've completed your education.

THE SECOND HALF OF PHASE 2

Now that you've made a plan and committed to it, it's time to start learning everything you can about your new world. If you're going the formal education route, start researching schools and applying. If you're educating yourself, work out your own curriculum and set deadlines for yourself. If you're going to learn by doing, find a mentor, join a team, and start learning the ropes.

Whether you're getting a formal education, educating yourself, or learning by doing, in the second half of Phase 2, you should: continue researching your new field, keep going to industry conferences, and find a mentor.

RESEARCH

No matter what industry you're entering, continue learning everything you can about it. Read your new field's articles and magazines, and constantly feed your mind with information about it. You need to be current on the latest trends so you can participate in relevant conversations. This way, you'll be able to ask smarter questions and demonstrate your seriousness to more senior people who can help or hire you. Whatever you want to do, hundreds—if not thousands—of people have done it before you. Learning from their experience means you don't have to make every available mistake yourself.

CONFERENCES

There are multiple conferences every year for every industry and many of the subspecializations in most of them. I swear I'm not taking a kickback from some conference-organizing organization, but I haven't found a better way to extend my knowledge and my network as effectively. More than once, I've been surprised by how willing people who would be very hard to contact otherwise are to sit and chat with an aspiring newbie or interested stranger. I recently had breakfast with an entrepreneur I'd never met who'd just sold his business for $8 billion—because we were both at the same conference, and I introduced myself.

MENTORS

If you can find someone willing to let you work alongside them, review your work, or tell you their story, you'll have a huge advantage over everyone who's blundering about trying to figure everything out for themselves. I honestly don't understand why more people don't seek out mentors. I suspect it's a confidence problem—either they have too much and are too proud to ask for advice and help, or they don't have enough to believe anyone further down the path would be interested in helping them. Either way, it's a mistake.

There may be people willing to mentor you out of the pure goodness of their hearts, but the best mentor-mentee relationships are ones of mutual benefit. One-sided relationships aren't psychologically healthy, and there's no reason for the completely altruistic mentor to stick around.

Mentors can give you direct hands-on experience and expertise that you can't get any other way, so no matter how else you're getting educated for your new adventure, a mentor has something unique and invaluable to offer. Respect that and go to them with something of value to offer in return.

FINDING A MENTOR

Here's what *not* to do: Don't call up someone and say, "Hey, can I pick your brain about [insert industry here]? Can I ask you how you do your job, and then also how I can get to do your job? Can you take some time out of your busy day to show me how to do all that stuff and maybe introduce me to more people who can help me, because I know you're a nice person, and I'm sure you have extra time to give me hours and hours of free education, right?"

Don't expect anyone to teach you an entire industry or spoon-feed you basics you could have learned from a book or YouTube.

No matter what you've been told, there absolutely are stupid questions. Don't ask them of potential mentors.

The right way to find a mentor will vary a bit depending on your field, but the basic premise is universal: make it reciprocal.

In my television career, I took the direct route. "I want to work with you. I'll work with you for free. I want to learn, but I also want to help. What do you need? Do you want me to scout for you? Want me to answer your phones?" If I hadn't done my research, I wouldn't have been able to anticipate pain points like scouting. I had no idea how to do it, but people in the industry might be willing to teach me if I was taking work off their plates.

In anesthesiology, mentorship is baked into the organizational structure. Your boss mentors you, and the value you add in return is learning how not to kill anyone on their watch.

The model is different in entrepreneurship, but it's another place where time and money can trade places. When you're just getting started, putting in unpaid time is a great way to bring value to a mentor. Later, it's possible to pay a mentor for their time by hiring their expertise directly or trading it for shares.

WARNING SIGNS

It's unusual to stay too long in Phase 2. Unlike the daydreaming and early dating excitement of Phase 1, Phase 2 feels more preparatory than playful. If fear starts interfering here, you can still stall out between making a commitment and starting to take action, but usually, when people do that, they drop back into Phase 1 because it's more fun.

Phase 2 is a great time to ask a friend to hold you accountable and start building the "just do it" habit you'll need as you move into Phase 3 because once the moon gets full, everything starts happening, usually all at the same time.

CHAPTER SUMMARY

In Phase 2, you commit to your reinvention and start taking concrete steps to make it happen. In the first half of Phase 2, you validate the realism of your reinvention by performing an inventory of your personal obligations, financial resources, and professional skills and by estimating the cost of the education (formal or informal) that you'll need. You then make a commitment to your reinvention and start your education ready to head into Phase 3, when you'll start living your new, reinvented life. Are you ready? It's time to strap yourself in and hit the gas!

Chapter 8

PHASE 3, EDUCATION

WHEN I FOUND OUT I'D DONE WELL ON THE MCAT, I BRIEFLY considered applying to medical school. I'd accumulated enough experience to realize that if, instead of a two-year master's program, I did four years of medical school, I'd be able to start making moderately decent money during my residency, after which I'd be a doctor. But I was honest with myself. I didn't like school well enough or want to be a doctor fiercely enough to make that a better choice than the shorter path to becoming an anesthetist.

It still took a big leap of faith for me to believe I could dramatically reinvent my life—that I could go from waiting tables to med school to a six-figure job. As I reached the end of Phase 2 of my second reinvention cycle, I had a clear vision of what I wanted to do next and a plan for getting there. I was nervous, but I had gathered my courage and felt ready to try.

But life throws unexpected curveballs at you, and as I was getting ready to move to Georgia for anesthesia school, my fourteen-year-old younger brother and my mentally ill mother both came to live with me. I didn't know how I could support them and go to grad school, but I was determined to make it work. I had to wait tables while at Emory (which was prohibited), but I graduated and began my new, reinvented life with a strong salary and hope for a brighter future. I mention this because it's important for you to know that you must push through obstacles and not let excuses get in the way of your success and goals. You can do it!

EDUCATION AND EXPERIENCE

In this chapter, I'll talk you through what it takes to transition fully into a reinvention. We'll take a deeper look at three different models of education—formal, apprenticeship, and self-directed—and I'll offer advice and tips for each. We'll then look at some of the dangers that can threaten your reinvention in this, its most intense phase.

FULL MOON, FULL PLATE

In Phase 3, you transition from the old to the new. You fully inhabit your reinvented career and enjoy the honeymoon. Be prepared for this to take time and patience. Most overnight successes are years in the making. Most businesses take five to seven years to get off the ground, so if you're still not turning a profit two years in, it may be time to pivot—but not quit. If you've committed to becoming a writer, you can't give up when your first screenplay doesn't sell.

The preparatory work you did in the first two phases will come in handy when you face the inevitable difficulties and setbacks of Phase 3. When you're exhausted, tap back into Phase

2's excitement and desire. Remind yourself how much you want this reinvention and how cool you once thought it'd be to do exactly what you're doing now. When you get discouraged, go back to the preparatory work you did in Phase 2 and let your past due diligence silence your present doubts.

If you're trying to build your new career while you're still working at your old one, you can't be precious about it. It's more like scrabbling at a sheer rock face for your next handhold without losing the one you've got than it is an elegant leap from one launching pad to another.

Keep in touch with your motivation. It's fine if money is your primary goal (it was for me when I committed to pursuing anesthesiology), but it shouldn't be the only one. You'll probably work close to the equivalent of two full-time jobs throughout Phase 3 since you'll need to both support and educate yourself. Some educational paths through Phase 3 may require you to take on debt. Others may start paying you from early on. That's great, but try to think of it as a bonus, not the main objective. It's best if you can put off burdening your new venture with the pressure of supporting you for the first few years.

Be scrappy, but don't be stupid. (I probably pushed the line between the two, driving out into the heart of Kentucky alone to drink moonshine with oil drillers.) Finance what you have to with loans or your credit card if that's what you've planned to do, but live without everything you don't need. Pay for airfare to a convention if it's the right place to meet people, but pack yourself some protein bars for breakfast to save the cost of a twenty-dollar hotel breakfast. Be brave and take risks, but don't do unrecoverable harm to yourself, your kids, or your bank account.

Phase 3 is undoubtedly intense, but it's only two or three years out of the eighty you get, and if you're energized by what you're trying to accomplish, it's not just doable and worth it; it will probably also make you happier than working just one job where you feel stuck.

FORMAL EDUCATION

If, after doing your research, you determine that an accredited degree program is the price of entry to your chosen career reinvention, but you don't enjoy school, do a little more research to determine if there's a two-year program that will still let you do something that excites you.

If, on the other hand, you can't pay for the education you need now, you can probably pay for it later. The government practically throws loan money at students. Why? Because they know it's a good investment. There are grants you don't have to pay back and low-interest loans that you eventually do, but not until you're out of school and established in your new career. Many of these loan and grant programs are based solely on need or merit and don't even check your credit score.

Finally, if the hurdle you must clear to launch into Phase 3 through formal education is admission to an accredited school, there are side doors into the fabled halls of academe. My college grades weren't great, but my time working with battered women balanced them out. Take a good look at your history, and reframe your experiences to help make the case that you'll be an asset to the school you've set your sights on.

The biggest shortcut is courage. If the school requires test scores, take the test before you decide you need to spend the first four months of Phase 3 studying. If you don't pass it on your first try, you can always study and retake it later. Likewise, don't wait until you look better on paper to apply. Apply first. If you don't get in, spend a semester doing the things that will make you a more attractive candidate, whether that's volunteering, interning, building a demo piece, or creating a portfolio. Then apply again.

EXPERIENCE

Don't expect your reinvention education to be like your college experience, especially if you're in an accelerated program. The two years I spent at Emory were some of the most excruciating of my life. The curriculum was intense, and the internships we were assigned as part of our education placed us at different hospitals at uniformly painful early hours.

But then you graduate.

One advantage of many of these formal educational programs is that they include job-placement support. I walked out of school into the second half of Phase 3—work that was tremendously exciting. And scary. I literally had people's lives in my hands. I was learning more every day than I'd learned in a week of school and making more money than I'd ever imagined growing up a street kid in Venice, California.

Perhaps best of all, with the great salary came great medical coverage, and I was able to get my mom the mental-health support she needed. She was formally diagnosed with paranoid schizophrenia and, after a little experimentation, got on a regimen of meds that made an enormous difference in her functioning. She lived with me until she died, but once stabilized, she was more of a support than a burden. All I needed to do was make sure she took her meds, and she was able to live with me and help parent my kids in ways she'd been unable to care for her own.

My starting salary in my first year out of school was almost three times my income from working two jobs the year before I moved to Georgia. It was the most money I'd ever had in my life.

Then, in my second year out of school, there was a shortage of anesthetists, and my salary went up by $20,000—a raise the size of my annual teacher's salary. The year after that, it went up by 50 percent to $150,000. By that point, three years in, I felt like I was getting into the routine of the job and getting steadily better at it. I started being assigned to harder rooms, working cardiac surgeries and other high-stakes procedures. My skills kept growing through my fourth and fifth years after school. It was great!

Predictably, that's when I started to get bored. Seven years into my second reinvention cycle, the honeymoon was over, and my interest and enthusiasm were starting to wane.

APPRENTICESHIP

There are formal apprenticeship programs, but if your reinvention plan calls for you to train under someone who doesn't have "teacher" or "instructor" as part of their job description, you're going to have to get out there and find them. It's not going to feel natural at first, but get out of your comfort zone and talk to people. Network.

BE VISIBLE

Do things you never thought you'd do—fly to LA or Cincinnati, Ohio. Go places you never would have thought to go, to meet with people and make connections. You'll be surprised how much faster you can succeed in any career just by going to all the industry-specific events and putting yourself out there.

If you want to break into music, try going to Nashville and hitting up all the country bars. Do open mics. Get your craft out there and start getting feedback. Put up a YouTube channel and make sure people hear your voice.

LEARN BY WATCHING

This was the educational path I took into television. I had a TV producer who mentored me and showed me, step by step, how to make a sizzle reel. After he sold a few of my tapes, I felt I'd provided enough value to ask him to start taking me on pitch meetings to learn that skill.

One day, he took me with him to pitch Animal Planet a tape I'd made about raccoon hunters and their dogs. I'd worked on it for weeks, researching the deeply weird sport of competition raccoon hunting. I'd gone to several of these events to interview the dog owners and film their pets chasing raccoons into trees. I was incredibly excited.

We had twenty minutes with an exec my mentor hadn't met before, and I was interested to see how he handled what was basically a cold call. We walked in and shook hands, and the exec, let's call him Steve, noticed my mentor's shoes.

"Hey, Brad, great shoes."

"Thanks! They're from this weird little brand out of Italy."

"Where'd you get them?"

Brad told him, and it turned out Steve shopped there too. They compared notes on when the store had sales and whether their great customer service was worth the markup over buying shoes online. They talked about other shoe stores and other shoe brands until I thought I might pull off my shoes and start beating Brad with them.

We only had twenty minutes, and ten minutes in, they were still talking about shoes! I'm honestly still surprised I didn't try saying something like "You know who else wears shoes? These guys with trained raccoon-hunting dogs!"

We still had seven minutes left when Steve sounded like he was done. "So, it was great getting to know you guys," he said. "Thanks for coming over. What do you have?"

I pounced. "A five-minute tape," I said. "Let me just show you these wonderful dogs. Their owners are real characters, and they compete in competitions..." I delivered the whole pitch before he got the tape into the machine. With five minutes left, he cued it up and watched it.

"This is great!" he said, standing up and shaking our hands. "I like this one." He walked us to the door. "I'll take it up the chain and see what we can do."

I was seething. "I can't believe you took my whole meeting talking about shoes!" I hissed on the way out of the building. "I didn't even get to show him my slides!"

"Whoa, whoa, what happened at the end of the meeting?" Brad said. "That was a sale, right?"

"Um," I said. "Yes?"

"Yeah."

"I'm just mad we didn't get to sell him on the show."

"Cherie," he grinned at me. "I was selling it the whole time. This business is all about relationships. It's about them thinking, *You're cool people, and I want to do business with you.* If they don't like the tape, they'll take the next pitch, but if they don't like you, they won't bite even if it's a great tape. And they won't talk to you next time. Steve's a low-paid minor exec. He sees slides all day long. But how many people will let him talk about shoes?"

We sold *Raccoon Hunters* to Animal Planet. It didn't make it to air, but the lesson I learned at that pitch meeting helped shape my success in TV, and I remembered it years later when I was building SnapNurse. And the only way I could have learned it was by being in the room and seeing it happen.

LEARN BY FAILING

On the apprenticeship educational path, you'll constantly be doing things you're entirely unqualified and untrained to do. This would be disastrous in anesthesiology, but it can feel every bit as fatal in television. No one dies, but you may feel like you want to.

My first pitch meetings in New York were truly awful. I was nervous and intimidated by everyone. I stumbled over my words. My mind blanked on questions I absolutely had answers for. I had some very bad meetings—so bad that the execs would criticize them while I was still in the room. One terrible early pitch taught me the lesson I shared in the last chapter: keep doing your research.

Very early on, I went in cold to a meeting with A&E Networks. I honestly have no idea why I thought it would be a good plan to show up and invent reality show concepts on the spot. It wasn't. This was my first connection to the network. I sat there and racked my brain. "Okay!" I said. "Here's my idea. There are these storage units, and they regularly get abandoned, so the rental companies sell whatever's in them at auction, and people bid not knowing what's inside. It could be a bunch of old clothes and yard tools or an antique car in pristine condition. So, then there's this big reveal after someone buys it when they open it up!"

Not too shabby for a spur-of-the-moment inspiration.

"Storage Wars," the exec said.

And before I could get excited that he'd come up with such a great name for what I'd just pitched, he added, very dryly, "It's in its second season."

If I'd done even a little research, I would have known what reality TV shows the network I was pitching already ran. Lesson learned. I never went in unprepared again.

RECOVER FROM FAILURE

I'd bombed my A&E meeting, and I knew it. I fessed up. "It's clear I don't have a pitch," I said. "So what is it? What's the show you'd love to have? What would you green-light immediately?"

It didn't take him a second. "The Olsen twins."

"Okay," I said. "But if I deliver a meeting with the Olsen twins, you have to continue taking my pitches, right?"

He agreed, and I went home and started calling every person I'd ever met in my life. "Hey, do you know the Olsen twins?" Unbelievably, an acquaintance of mine had gone to college with the woman who was now the CEO of the Olsens' clothing company, and after a great deal more calling and cajoling, I ended up orchestrating the very first meeting with the Olsen twins and A&E Networks.

CAPITALIZE ON WINS

Having delivered the Olsen twins, I felt like I had redeemed myself enough to ask the same guy what he wanted next. "Just do a couple of interviews and send them my way," he said. "I'll take a look and tell you if you're on the right track." I did, and as I started to bring him value, it created enough trust that I could reach back out—not every day, but every few weeks—and ask him what he was looking for.

I took full advantage of his willingness to look at interviews I recorded too. I'd wake up early on the weekends and drive all over the South looking for interesting characters and stories. In Alabama, I found a community making arguably the worst zombie film ever made, and a separate group of guys going down to the Amazon jungle to mine for gold. There were people in Kentucky drilling for oil in people's backyards, and folks in Montana digging sapphires out of enormous rock piles. In some church denominations, families participated in a spelling bee-like competition in which they were given a Bible chapter and verse to recite rather than a word to spell. In Ohio, I found a neighborhood where seven of the married couples—including a teacher, a police officer, and a hairdresser—were all swingers. I was having a ball! My shows aired on the History Channel, TLC International, TLC, the Discovery Channel, SYFY, and A&E Networks.

Along the way, my new mentor introduced me to Red Line Films, a production company, and the team there became mentors as well. They helped me develop the skills I needed to grow and sell the shows I was finding. They spent the money to flesh out my pitches with great music and better production values. They taught me how to get the best sound bites out of interview subjects and edit the tape to get in the juiciest bits while still telling a coherent story in the three minutes we had allotted. I brought them shows on which they made money, and they gave me a great education. I loved working with Red Line Films. We had a kind of collaborative magic and ended up selling seven shows together.

KEEP LEARNING

Because the value I had to offer was, at least initially, coming up with great ideas, characters, and stories, I spent a lot of my time chasing those down. But I wasn't the only one out there in the field, and I identified my greatest point of vulnerability as the time it took to get an idea from my head to the people who could pitch it up the chain. I'd go out, find the people, do the interviews, and then send all my materials to a production company and wait—sometimes as long as three weeks—for them to edit the tape. It made me nuts! Anyone else could scoop all that work out from under me if they had the same idea and got a sizzle reel together and in front of the decision-makers first.

Of course, everyone else in my position faced the same delays, but I was restless, so I started sitting in with the editors while they edited my tapes—not to breathe down their necks, but to learn. I supplemented that education with self-directed education, learning more about editing videos online. Finally, I made (what was for me at the time) a big investment in my reinvention, bought an industry-standard video-editing software license, and started cutting my own tapes together.

Once, I edited four reels in a single day and sent them all in. I got a slightly perplexed response back. "You don't understand," they told me. "This isn't how TV works. Nobody turns tapes in this fast. But these are great, so we're going to take them."

As Dr. Sackett, who I mentioned in Chapter 2, pointed out in his argument that experts should exit their fields of expertise, it's often people new to an industry who advance it the most. I didn't question the assumptions so much as fail to recognize them. It was as simple as realizing that I could do my job more efficiently if I taught myself a skillset from a different job and started knocking out tapes overnight. I wasn't trying to be revolutionary; I was just learning everything I could. When you're new and hungry, you can often move through the ranks more quickly than someone who's come up within the system adopting the limitations everyone accepts without really knowing they're there.

KEEP IMPROVING

I kept upping my game and improving my skills, getting very good at finding fascinating characters. Eventually, I got to the point that I didn't need to travel so much to get the supporting interviews and started doing them over Skype. It took a little work to ensure everyone in a group was in the frame, but I got to the point that I could get everything I needed recorded online, edit the Skype interview into a compelling sizzle reel, and sell a show that way.

THE HONEYMOON

One advantage of the apprenticeship model is that, unlike formal education, the fun can start almost immediately. I loved this learning process from the first pitch meeting I sat in on with Mark at the Peachtree Film Festival. But the demarcation you get between the first and second stages of Phase 3 in formal education, when you graduate to full-time work from full-time learning, isn't as clear in this model.

I had to keep working my anesthesia job, ducking outside on my lunch break to take a call with a network and then running back to the operating room, where the surgeons would mock me for what I was trying to do. I had a great job at the hospital. Why was I investing time and money up front on projects hoping to be paid down the road if they sold?

As I proved my value, I started to get a monthly stipend from a production company, but even when I was regularly selling shows, I wasn't reliably making enough to quit my other job. It wasn't until I'd built a reputation as a great development producer with big hits on the History and Discovery Channels and with other production companies trying to hire me away from Red Line that they put me on salary. Even then, I hung on to my anesthesiology job for a bit.

By that time, I was well and truly bored with anesthesia. I would have been miserable without the exciting TV work to keep my energy up. The people I worked with didn't understand what I was doing or why (more on that in the Dangers section), and they'd mock me about it. "One day," I'd tell them, "I'm going to leave. Eventually, I'm going to make it in TV and do that full-time."

They'd just laugh at me. "Oh sure, okay. You tell us when that's going to happen."

In that funny way life occasionally has of goosing you at well-timed moments, I was back in the OR one day shortly after Red Line had started paying me a salary that came very close to matching what I was making at the hospital. A new hire came in and sat down next to me in the break room. She'd done one of her student rotations with us a year ago. "Still here?" she asked with a sympathetic smile. "I remember you. You swore you'd leave here one day and work in TV."

"You know what? You're right," I said. "That 'one day' is today." And I put in my two weeks' notice. That was a very good day!

DANGERS

Two of the three dangers of the apprenticeship model of education are common to any reinvention: stress and opposition. The third, working on spec, is unique to it.

Working on Spec

Like the traditional craftsperson's apprentice who made shoes or barrels on which the master made all the profit until the training was complete, doing work for free or in the hopes that it may sell one day is standard in this educational model. Screenwriters and novelists spend months or years completing their scripts and books in the hope that once finished, they'll beat the enormous odds and sell.

If your reinvention requires you to build an audience for your music or an inventory for your Etsy store, you'll put in many hours before you get much money out of your new reinvention. Framing this to yourself as the tuition or cost of your education in your new field can help, but it's important to be mentally prepared and to have an income stream you can count on to meet your obligations. If you don't, it can be very tempting to take the kind of shortcuts in quality that end up keeping you from ever recouping your investment.

Stress

I'll talk more about stress later, but since the apprenticeship model usually requires you to work the equivalent of two full-time jobs, the sheer time pressure you're under during these years is certain to be stressful. Your enthusiasm for the new life you're building mitigates a lot of that stress, but it doesn't make what you're trying to do easy.

Opposition

As I mentioned in Chapter 4, not everyone reacts well to change. If you're doing something different either from what you are used to or from what everyone else is doing (or both), you will get some pushback. I encountered that with every one of my reinventions, but it was nastiest while I was working in anesthesiology and learning the ropes of TV.

Maybe it had something to do with the rigid hierarchy of the medical field, where doctors feel entitled to treat their "underlings" with disrespect, but I took a lot of abuse from surgeons about what I was doing. They didn't understand why I was doing it, but they always asked about it. Every Monday morning, it was always the first topic of conversation. "Hey Cherie, what crazy adventure did you go on this weekend?"

I'd tell them the story of heading out to Jasper, Alabama, where they're filming a zombie movie, and everyone would love the story. They'd laugh at the funny parts and shake their heads at the strangeness of humanity. They loved the stories, but when they were done enjoying them, they'd always add something cutting. Usually, it was "You're so crazy!" or "You're out of your mind. It's ridiculous. Why would you want to leave anesthesiology?"

I've encountered this kind of response with almost every one of my reinventions, but it was particularly unkind with this one. Calling someone crazy is just insulting. It implies there's something wrong with you for wanting to try something new or that the only reason anyone would want to make a significant change is that they're having a mental breakdown or midlife crisis. Somehow, they think it's saner to stay in a job they hate and take antidepressants.

I'm sure part of it is the human tendency to judge what we don't understand. The doctors I worked with didn't understand why I wanted to spend my nights and weekends working to build a new career. Maybe some of them were jealous of the excitement I had in my life and the interesting stories it gave me to tell. Maybe some of them were threatened by it and trying to discourage me.

There's also a kind of sometimes hidden, sometimes overt sexism to calling something a woman's doing "crazy" or "silly." I never heard anyone say the same thing about a man who was trying to get a startup off the ground. I think there's a lingering image of women as fragile and neurotic. Women "get the vapors" when we're overwhelmed instead of "being under a lot of pressure" the way men might be. If we're very excited and energized by something, we're "hysterical" (a word that comes from the

Greek word for womb, and that you'll still never see applied to men except as a modifier to "funny").

I usually laughed it off, but it was actually very upsetting. Worse, it can make you start to doubt yourself. I remember wondering if they were right. Maybe it really *was* crazy for me to want something more for myself. Maybe there was something wrong with me that I was bored.

There wasn't. I hadn't seen the research then, but I have now, and it's clear that almost everyone starts to get bored after five years. It's the norm, not an aberration. If you know what's coming, you're not being mentally ill to start planning for that inevitable drop in interest and satisfaction. People who want to change careers aren't just losing their minds. In fact, if we accept Einstein's definition of insanity—doing the same thing over and over and expecting a different result—then staying in a job that no longer challenges you and expecting it to suddenly become fulfilling is crazier than trying something new.

The ten-year reinvention cycle I'm advocating here is the opposite of crazy. It's a careful, controlled, deliberate way of continuing to learn and grow throughout your working life. Over the years and through multiple reinventions, I came to redefine their "crazy" as "brave." It is scary to try new things, but I wasn't taking big risks. I was taking big adventures.

My mother had serious mental-health issues. I know what "crazy" looks like, and it doesn't look like finding a new career that excites you, researching, making a plan, committing to that plan, educating yourself, and transitioning into full-time work in a new field. Is doing that normal? No. But I never aspired to normal. I want interesting.

If you're in the third phase of a reinvention, working two jobs and feeling stressed, and people are telling you you're crazy, you aren't. What you are is extraordinary—as in more than ordinary. If a man were doing what you're doing, they'd call it brave or ambitious. Every time you hear "crazy," translate it as "adventurous."

You can also take a page from the "crazy" Ruth Bader Ginsburg, who credited her mother-in-law with the advice that "it helps sometimes to be a little deaf."[24] Personally, after having had "crazy" lobbed at me by people who didn't understand what I was doing and at my mother, who was legitimately mentally ill, I'd like to humbly suggest we reclaim another old word for people whose ambition and enthusiasm may seem unhinged or excessive to more pedestrian minds—lunatic.

If you're living your life in ten-year reinvention cycles, the old, late-thirteenth-century definition of "lunatic" ("affected with periodic insanity dependent on the changes of the moon") seems fairly accurate. That the word comes from the even older Latin *lunaticus*, which meant "moon-struck," taken from the name of the Roman moon goddess, Luna, suits me too.

Call us crazy? From now on, I'll hear "goddess," thank you very much.

SELF-EDUCATION

I augmented my apprenticeship with additional education. I taught myself how to edit tapes and paid someone for lessons in shooting videos. I'm currently pursuing a self-education program to learn more about AI. Self-education can be a great path to reinvention if you have a lot of financial and personal obligations and not much in the way of available resources, or

---

24 Mark Murphy, "Ruth Bader Ginsburg Delivered the Best Career Advice You'll Ever Hear, in Just One Sentence," Forbes, September 20, 2020, https://www.forbes.com/sites/markmurphy/2020/09/20/ruth-bader-ginsburg-delivered-the-best-career-advice-youll-ever-hear-in-just-one-sentence/?sh=4da7bb2e113f.

if your reinvention is closer to evolution than beginning from scratch in an entirely new field.

If you're working in an industry that you enjoy but are starting to get restless, you can put together an educational program for yourself to learn the skills you'd need to move into a management position or get promoted. That could look like anything from taking online courses in leadership to reading up on etiquette.

When I decided I wanted a job in TV, all I knew was that the entire film and television industry was exciting to me. When I met Mark at the Peachtree Film Festival and realized the demand for reality TV concepts, I started educating myself by watching reality TV. It wasn't something I'd seen a lot, and frankly, I didn't care all that much about it, but if I wanted to sell it, I needed to understand why people found it compelling. I watched for trends in what got picked up and what was successful with audiences.

WARNING SIGNS

The work of Phase 3 is all the work all the time, and the corresponding warning signs, unsurprisingly, are burnout and fatigue. I was completely exhausted, but it wasn't until the coincidental return of a nursing student that I finally quit my safety job to go full-time into something I loved. Don't let fear keep you here longer than necessary.

The intensity of Phase 3 can be overwhelming. If you don't have much experience with success, imposter syndrome can kick in, and all the fears and lack of confidence you put behind you to start your reinvention can reemerge. The same techniques work, but just in case you need to hear it directly, you deserve to enjoy the rewards of your hard work. You're skillful enough and safe enough to take that final step into the light of your success.

CHAPTER SUMMARY

In Phase 3, you gain the education and experience you need to transition between your old life and your reinvented one. It's an intense and sometimes difficult span of years since you're often living both lives simultaneously, but you're well-prepared, and it's worth it!

The formal education route can accelerate the work of Phase 3 if you enjoy school and can afford to take the time and pay the price. Loans and grants can help, and there are often side doors into programs. If you're picking up your experience and education through an apprenticeship, you'll learn by doing, watching others, failing, and recovering. Be sure you're building relationships and providing value. With self-education, create your own curriculum based on the skills you'll need, and leverage online resources.

This will be the most challenging phase of your reinvention. You may need to work a full-time job to support yourself while also putting in a forty-hour week working on your education and experience, and the people around you may not understand your efforts. See their opposition as confirmation that you're doing something extraordinary.

It won't be easy, but persevere, and you'll enter Phase 4 fully transitioned into an exciting and interesting life doing something you love!

Chapter 9

PHASE 4, ACHIEVEMENT

AFTER THE FIRST LUNATIC YEARS AT SNAPNURSE, ONE OF our investors was so thrilled with our progress that he gifted us with the use of his private jet to go anywhere in the US. I took the entire SnapNurse executive team to the St. Regis in Aspen to celebrate our success.

And there I was, that lost, LA street-urchin girl, hosting ten of my work colleagues and best friends in a private jet with its own air hostess.

We all kept reminding each other, "We're in a private jet!"

The air hostess came by. "Would you like warm cookies?"

"Yes, we want warm cookies!"

"Would you like champagne?"

"Yes, we want champagne!"

I'd set out to have an interesting life, and now it was interesting with champagne and cookies!

SUCCESS AND STAGNATION

In this chapter, we come full circle. I'll remind you to enjoy the success you've worked so hard to achieve and talk about what I believe is the proper work of Phase 4—mentoring the young, remembering the past, and watching the future. Phase 4 is wonderful, but it doesn't last forever. Time keeps moving, and cycles keep turning, so we'll finish this, our last chapter, by talking about ways you can skip right over the difficult Phase 0 and get going on your next great reinvention.

THE HONEYMOON

When you've transitioned to working full-time in the job you once daydreamed about, take the time to really enjoy it. You can do this while you're still working full tilt, but don't forget to notice that right now, the fun is *really* fun. Congratulate yourself on having done what you set out to do, and bank the confidence you've earned. Add this cycle's achievements to your mental list of things that prove you can do big, brave things. You'll need it when you start the next cycle!

The beginning of Phase 4, when you're well-established but still learning and growing, is a great time to enjoy your success and share it. It's the ideal time to mentor others the way you were mentored and do for others what you wished someone had done for you. As Édith Piaf put it, "When you've reached the top, send the elevator back down."

BE A MENTOR

When my first career dream of becoming a doctor lost out to my lack of confidence, a young person's distorted sense of time, and a career counselor's bad advice, I got a little lost. I spent some time in careless fun, relaxing after the stress of being on my own while working and going to school. But as I cycled into the lack of fulfillment in what I was doing, the fun wasn't fun anymore, and I found myself stuck and lost.

The newspaper ad for a house manager at a homeless shelter jump-started my first reinvention cycle, and working at the Sheepfold taught me the rewards of mentorship. Part of my job was working with the battered women who stayed in our safe houses, and I applied the principles they taught me to pass on to the women in my own life. Counseling them helped me figure out myself.

I helped them find work and got their kids registered in school. I made sure they all had enough to eat. I also learned what the fear of being unable to support yourself can do to a woman. We only had a 25 percent success rate. It was just too hard for the women who came to us running for their lives not to go back to the men who beat them. And that taught me something too. It reinforced my need to be financially independent and showed me how childhood trauma can replay itself in your adult life if you don't work to get on top of it.

But I never really got out of the reality-checking of Phase 2. The pay was terrible. Most of the work was cooking and cleaning—not that different from what I was already doing waiting tables—and I found it depressing. I went back into Phase 1's daydreaming and research and took a teaching job. I did, however, get one full-moon moment out of my time at the Sheepfold that crystallized the importance and rewards of being a mentor. A year or two after I quit, I was walking back to my car at midnight after finishing a shift at the pizza restaurant. Out of the dark came a voice. "Cherie, is that you?"

One of the women I'd worked with at the Sheepfold had recognized me across the empty parking lot and came running over to say hello. "I just want you to know," she told me, "I never went back to [name of abuser]."

"That's great!" I said, "You beat the odds!"

"I know," she beamed. "And I got my old job back, and the kids are doing great, and I just wanted to tell you I never could have stood on my own without you and the Sheepfold. You got me back on my feet. I'm super grateful. Thank you!"

The rewards of mentorship may be delayed, and they may never be external, but they're real and mean a lot. Human beings are meant to help each other out.

That said, I've seen successful businesspeople collect board seats and mentees like trophies. I've been helped too much by mentors to take the role lightly. I believe mentors have responsibilities to their mentees that extend beyond just giving them advice, so if I invest in a mentor-mentee relationship, I invest financially. This gives me some skin in the game, assures my mentee that I have something to win or lose with them, and keeps our relationship from being one-sided.

I'm also very careful not to give advice just because it's flattering to be asked for it. I'm happy to listen over a cup of coffee and offer my personal perspective, but if I'm going to give business advice, I'll only give it where I know the industry or issue.

As an example, at the moment, I'm actively mentoring two people: my brother and a female entrepreneur. I've invested money in my brother's startup. I'm comfortable advising him on ways to structure and scale the business and how to find good legal help, and I give him pointers on dealing with HR in California. I'm not going to give him advice on embryo storage because I don't know anything about it.

When I've been approached to mentor people whose space I don't know, I believe it's my responsibility to tell them that. If I can, I may point them to someone who knows the industry, but I'm not qualified to help someone start a home-healthcare staffing company. Sure, I know nurses and staffing, but I don't know home care at all, and I might do more harm than good if I make assumptions about how it works based on my experience.

On the other hand, I have taken on mentoring a woman-owned startup that's creating a staffing platform in an industry that's so different from nursing that I'm clear on where I can be helpful and where I can't. As with my brother's company, I've also backed the company financially so that she and I understand that I have a vested interest in helping connect her to other investors and making sure she knows what she's doing and does it all correctly.

If you've reached the fourth phase of your reinvention and people are asking for your mentorship, don't think of it as doing them a favor. If you believe you can be of real help to them, are able to give good advice, and are willing to invest, then great. If not, even if they're offering you free shares, be aware that joining a board might be more of a disservice and that sometimes, the most helpful thing you can do is decline.

DO FOR OTHERS

When I started SnapNurse, helping women wasn't one of my primary objectives the way it was when I took the house manager job at the Sheepfold. The work I did counseling battered women was rewarding, and I know I helped at least a percentage of the families who came through the program, but I ended up being able to do much more for many more women as the CEO of a billion-dollar company.

I never forgot what it was like to be the single mother of two kids, trying to make ends meet while working two jobs. So, when COVID-19 forced all the SnapNurse office staff to start working from home, and I noticed my credentialing manager was looking a little rough around the edges, I thought I had a good idea why. She was a powerhouse, amazingly fast and good at her job, but she had three kids under five, and they were stuck at home with her. They'd climb on her during Zoom calls and start screaming out of sheer boredom.

I got her on a video call and leveled with her. "You need someone in your house to help."

"I know!" she said. "I can't even go to the bathroom by myself. But I ran the numbers, and I can't afford someone to come work for us full-time to manage the kids and the house."

"How much would it cost?"

"Two thousand dollars a month."

"Do it," I told her. "I'll pay for it."

She just stared into the camera. "Are you serious?"

"Yes, I'm serious. It's worth it to me to have you working at capacity and not being pulled in seven directions at the same time. Hire someone, and we'll cover the cost in the form of a raise. But you must use the raise to get someone in your house." I was just being practical, but she started to cry. She thought I'd scheduled the call to dress her down for being so frazzled.

The person she hired changed everything for her. She could focus on her work during the day and sit down with her husband and kids to a healthy, home-cooked dinner at night. She was more relaxed and focused and better at her job. It made such an enormous difference in how she felt and performed that I got myself an assistant too, and extended the offer first to all the female execs in the company and then to all the female managers.

Because I knew how much trouble I and many other women have spending money on themselves, I set up the home-support benefit to be separate from salary. It wasn't a "work harder, and

I'll pay you more" deal. Instead, we earmarked up to an additional $50,000 a year for each of our executives and managers to hire someone to take their kids to soccer practice, do the laundry, make dinner, or ensure they woke up every morning to a clean kitchen. They didn't have to take the benefit if they didn't need it, but they couldn't get it as cash. It was designed to equalize the invisible costs many women pay to work.

We made a distinction between meaningful and nonmeaningful tasks. I wasn't paying people to miss their kids' dance recitals or bedtimes, but to free up the time they spent doing the work that needs to get done that not only doesn't enrich but often detracts from the important relationships they have in their lives. I wanted them to have more time with their partners and children without the distractions that also distracted them at work.

It's another time people called something I did crazy, but this time they meant it with love and usually said it in tears, as in "You have no idea what this means to my family. It's crazy how much of a difference it makes." I was okay with that.

I know from personal experience how many ways being a mother can count against you in the professional world. Companies are reluctant to hire women whose résumés show a gap in their work history during the years their children were small. They resist letting women work part-time and ask coded interview questions for "Do you have children?" like "Can you travel?"

By removing those barriers, I was able to hire an amazing group of talented and hard-working women with a ferocious loyalty to the company. I regularly hear other CEOs complain about how hard it is to find qualified and loyal employees, and I'm frankly baffled why it doesn't occur to more of them to create a woman- and family-friendly environment. It's not just the more ethical thing to do; it's the more profitable one.

This is a bit of mentorship and advice-giving I hand out for free and to anyone: if you or someone who works for you is running around stressed out by obligations and weighed down with guilt, hire a personal home assistant. The difference it makes is immediate and profound.

BE A PERSON

When I was retiring from SnapNurse, one of the things that surprised me was how many people thanked me for things that it never would have occurred to me not to do. I like people, and I want to work with people I like. Apparently, it was a strange thing, as a CEO, to have your employees over to your house for dinner or to get to know them well, but I wouldn't want to do business any other way.

During COVID-19, when hospital nurses went on strike, SnapNurse would provide the staffing to ensure patients were cared for. It was always an extremely stressful and hectic operation, and I never missed one. I rolled up my sleeves and helped organize alongside everyone else. And it always surprised people. "You're the CEO, and you're here, doing this?"

Well, where else would I be? I was there because I wanted to see my people succeed and to help make sure everything worked out. I never thought I was better than the nurse working in the field—because I was that nurse.

Whether you rise through the ranks or start at the top and build a business under you, don't forget what it was like when you were in the positions your people now occupy. You may be signing their paychecks, but you'll sit down to dinner just like they do at the end of the day.

EVERYTHING NEW IS OLD AGAIN

And then you find yourself mad about eucalyptus. In late Phase 4, it starts getting dark again. You get bored and impatient. At this point, the work is to keep one eye on the horizon and the other on yourself. Try to recognize the old familiar feeling of when a reinvention is coming to an end and a new cycle is beginning. Don't get discouraged. This is a natural process.

WATCH THE FUTURE

This is no time to get out of the habit of reading the trades and watching the trends. When you go to conferences (you're still going to conferences, aren't you?), attend any talk with the word "disruption" in the title. Google "disruption in [your industry]." Whether you're the CEO or working on the front lines of your new industry, even when everything is going great and you're enjoying the honeymoon of being new enough to be excited but not so new that you're still working two jobs, you need to keep an eye on the horizon line of the economic landscape.

By my seventh year in television, I was getting bored with editing tapes and sick of selling only one in every eight I made. Then it was one in ten. I looked around the industry and saw the demand for reality TV was drying up.

Networks were ordering fewer new shows and doubling down on existing properties. The audience for *Duck Dynasty* had dropped from eleven million to two million viewers. It wasn't going to get canceled, but nobody was rolling out other duck shows or different dynasties. Some new shows were still selling but more slowly and for less money. Others were getting canceled before they made it to air. I started thinking it was time to leave.

Entrepreneurs need to keep an eye on the future of their

industry and their business. Most startups fail, so if you're running out of money, it's time to pivot your company or consider selling it so you have enough resources left to try something else.

Even if your company is hugely successful, you'll still get bored, and the world will still change. I'd started SnapNurse before the pandemic, but it was still a small company when COVID-19 hit. Suddenly, the demand for nurses was so high and the need so critical that the government was forced to innovate. It opened licensure between states and lowered credentialing requirements, allowing for quicker placement of nurses.

As the pandemic ended and we had time to catch our breath, it was unclear whether the contracts we had were COVID-19 contracts or ones that would continue post-pandemic. Worse, in the clash between the old and new government processes, I saw that the old was winning. The industry regulations were reverting like a dog returning to its vomit, and I started thinking things would change quickly.

WATCH YOURSELF

As you reach the end of Phase 4, usually around seven to ten years in, the fun stops being fun. Just waking up and getting to do your job isn't thrilling anymore. You're no longer putting your whole self into your work, and the work no longer asks as much of you. You've gotten too good at it. It's a grown routine. Maybe your energy is low, or you're getting irritable. Maybe you wake up dreading your day, feeling underpaid or underempowered, or find time is starting to drag. Are you bored? Are you boring? Do you recognize this list of classic Phase 0 symptoms from Chapter 1? As you reach the end of Phase 4, you can easily get stuck in this dark place and that dull job for years. Or you can start a new cycle.

Tolstoy defined boredom as "the desire for desire." When a job that used to challenge you becomes mindlessly routine, it's time to go desire-finding again. Go back to asking yourself questions and exploring your interests.

When I saw reality TV was on the wane, I started my brainstorming by talking to my brother. He lived in California and was keenly aware of the gathering tech boom. I started doing some research and thought tech was interesting. My next reinvention cycle started with some frankly very bad startup ideas. After a few educational try-fail cycles, I finally picked up some momentum and kept moving through the next three phases with SnapNurse.

You can start daydreaming about what could come next even before you're cranky and bored, but what's most critical here is to recognize what you're feeling as symptomatic of the phase you're in.

Of course, the cycles aren't always as neatly progressive as I've described. Sometimes you reach Phase 4 on fire instead of in the warm glow of a professional honeymoon. My mantra in these times is "It was a good run." If you did the research and reality-testing work of Phase 2 and went through Phase 3's education, you took a smart gamble that didn't pan out the way you'd hoped, but you learned a lot, and you'll approach the next cycle better prepared and more informed. That's a good run.

REST AND RECOVERY

It's perfectly fine to relax into the routine of early Phase 4 for a while if you're enjoying it, the future looks stable, and the fun is still fun. But when you start getting bored, get that reinvention cycle cranking again.

WARNING SIGNS

The biggest danger of Phase 4 is getting stuck here either through inertia or exhaustion. If you're tired, rest, but if you're stuck, it's probably too much fear or the inertia of not enough. For a dog sitting on a not-sharp-enough nail, the upsides of success can be very hard to risk on the chance of change.

Take courage from the fact that you've already completed at least one reinvention cycle. Even if it didn't work out the way you planned, you can feel proud of having taken your life by its ears and pointed it in a direction that excited you. Now it's time to do it again!

Another danger that shows up in Phase 4 surprises a lot of people, but I see it over and over. People who could barely catch their breath in Phase 3 finally hit success and suddenly don't know what to do with themselves. It's not that they're bored. It happens more quickly than that. It can happen just days after they achieve the crowning milestone they've been striving to reach.

I think this happens when the source of excitement that moves people out of Phase 1 and into action isn't the work itself but what it represents. If you want to move up the ladder at work or start a business not because you think doing those things would be interesting and fun but because they'd say something about you or prove something to someone else (yes, probably your dad), then when you finally reach that goal and find it doesn't solve the underlying problem, it can be devastating. I've heard way too many stories about rich and successful entrepreneurs who ended up as suicides.

Believe it or not, you'll face some of the same old BS in Phase 4 that you did in Phase 3. If your career reinvention has been a success, people are going to tell you you're crazy to leave. I heard it more than I care to remember. "But you're the CEO! You made it! You're crazy to walk away from all that."

I wasn't. I'm not. I'm brave. You are too.

CHAPTER SUMMARY

In the honeymoon period of Phase 4, you've fully established yourself in your reinvented career and can enjoy your success. This is a great time to be a mentor to others. Investing time and money shows commitment and gives you some skin in the game. It's also a time to do for others what you wish had been done for you. As you take some well-earned victory laps, remember your past and stay grounded. Don't let success change how you treat people. And don't allow yourself to be lulled into complacency. Keep one eye on the future of your industry for signs of disruption, and one eye on yourself so you know when it's time to start desire-finding and exploring again.

CONCLUSION

THE NEXT ADVENTURE

A TEN-YEAR REINVENTION ISN'T RIGHT FOR EVERYONE—
some people have great forty-year runs in the same career—but
I think it's a better fit for more people than most realize. Certainly, for anyone who feels bored or stuck in their job, whether
because it pays too well to leave or because they doubt their
ability to do something else, thinking about life as a series of
cycles can be freeing.

After a few reinvention cycles, you'll learn to identify the
way your warning signs manifest, but for most people, there's
some combination of feeling irritable, no longer enjoying the
things that you used to find fun, low energy, being bored or
boring, facing the morning with exhaustion or dread, feeling
underpaid and undervalued, and experiencing time as sluggish
or even stopped.

But these Phase 0 symptoms aren't typically enough to shake
people out of thinking of life as too short to have more than one
career path. Once you realize how long life actually is, you start

treating time as an investment and thinking of life as a series of ten-year cycles. Ten years is a long time to spend in any profession, and being able to spot the signs that a cycle is coming to an end allows you to start preparing for the next one before the current one ends. By overlapping the end of one cycle with the start of the next, you set yourself up for an interesting life with fewer regrets. You'll also protect your income-earning potential, be more pleasant to be around, and increase your happiness, luck, charisma, and success!

With so much to recommend it, this regular reinvention process can sound simple and easy, but people often struggle to get out of Phase 0 and into action. The fear of loss, failure, change, and judgment can combine with the sunk-cost fallacy, social conditioning, and the legacy of trauma to keep people stuck. To get around fear and build up courage, I recommend getting in touch with the energy of desire and building up your confidence by looking at all you've already finished, accomplished, and learned. You can also deliberately generate more confidence by doing some "adventure training" and by taking baby steps toward your reinvention.

Phase 0 is emotionally difficult, but Phase 1 of the ten-year reinvention cycle is so much fun! In this discovery phase, you ask yourself desire-finding questions and do desire-finding exercises. You explore and try out your new ideas in low-stakes and then slightly higher-stakes "dates." You also keep an eye out for the warning signs that you've stayed too long in this phase and prepare to make the commitment that signals the move into Phase 2.

Phase 2 is all about setting yourself up for success. You've narrowed your options and can test your reinvention plans against reality. You inventory your resources and assess the education or training you'll need. With that work done, you commit to your reinvention, find a mentor, and start ramping up for Phase 3.

Phase 3 is the most intense—full of the energy and excitement that comes with finally getting to work on making your dreams into reality. It can be overwhelming. Often, you'll be working two full-time jobs or doing the functional equivalent by going to school. In Phase 3, you'll climb a steep learning curve by educating yourself, becoming an apprentice, or enrolling in a formal educational program. If you're starting a new business, it may feel like you're working three jobs, putting double time into your fledgling company while holding down a "regular" job for its steady income.

Phase 3 comes to an end as you reach success (or fail to and cut your losses). In Phase 4, you can take some time to enjoy the fruits of your hard work or lick your wounds, recovering from the hectic pace you maintained in Phase 3. This is an ideal time to send the elevator back down, become a mentor, and help out people earlier in the reinvention cycle. But it's also time to be looking ahead to your next reinvention. As the energy wanes from the last cycle, once you're rested, you can ease into the discovery work of Phase 1 and avoid the irritation and boredom of Phase 0.

Living your life in a series of ten-year reinvention cycles may not be the easiest way to go through your long life, but it may be the most interesting. I also think it's the kindest thing you can do for the people closest to you and for yourself. Life is long. You have plenty of time to start working on your next phase or decade of life. Be brave and go for it!

ABOUT THE AUTHOR

CHERIE KLOSS is the founder and former chief executive officer of SnapNurse, a healthcare tech–enabled staffing platform. The company has grown exponentially since its founding in 2017. The company logged meteoric growth from 2018 to 2021 with a 146,319 percent revenue growth (from $3 million to $1.2 billion) and ranked number two on Inc 5000's fastest growing companies list in 2022. She won Ernst and Young's National Entrepreneur of the Year in 2021.

Cherie, who served as an anesthetist for eighteen years, founded SnapNurse to offer a more efficient ecosystem for healthcare systems and nurses to work together. She realized how broken the industry's credentialing and hiring process was, so she created the company to ultimately help solve the world's critical nursing shortage.

Before starting her healthcare technology business, Cherie was an accomplished unscripted reality TV producer, inking thirty-eight network deals with major cable networks such as

A&E, TLC, History Channel, Discovery Channel, Animal Planet, AMC, and the SYFY network.

Her multistoried career path, which includes being a social worker, teacher, anesthetist, TV producer, and tech entrepreneur, is captured in this book. She was a single mom and now is an empty nester with two grown children currently in college.

Cherie is currently an angel investor, start-up advisor, and surfer living in San Clemente, California.

Cherie holds a BS in biology and premed from Westmont College and a master's degree from Emory University School of Medicine.